The Spanish Inquisition

The Spanish Inquisition

Susan McCarthy Melchiore

CHELSEA HOUSE PUBLISHERS
Philadelphia

CHELSEA HOUSE PUBLISHERS

Editor in Chief Sally Cheney
Director of Production Kim Shinners
Production Manager Pamela Loos
Art Director Sara Davis
Production Editor Diann Grasse

Staff for THE SPANISH INQUISITION

Senior Editor John Ziff
Layout 21st Century Publishing and Communications, Inc.

First Printing

1 3 5 7 9 8 6 4 2

The Chelsea House World Wide Web address is
http://www.chelseahouse.com

Library of Congress Cataloging-in-Publication Data

Melchiore, Susan McCarthy
    The Spanish Inquisition / Susan McCarthy Melchiore
        p. cm. — (Great disasters, reforms, and ramifications)
    Includes bibliographical references and index.
    Summary: Describes the activities of the Spanish Inquisition,
which used questioning, torture, and execution to battle heresy
both in Spain and in the New World.
    ISBN 0-7910-6327-5 (alk. paper)
    1. Inquisition—Spain—Juvenile literature. 2. Spain—
Church history—Juvenile literature. [1. Inquisition—Spain.
2. Spain—Church history.] I. Title II. Series.

BX1735 .M46 2001
272'.2'0946—dc21   2001042374

Contents

GREAT DISASTERS
REFORMS and RAMIFICATIONS

Jill McCaffrey
National Chairman
Armed Forces Emergency Services
American Red Cross

Introduction

Disasters have always been a source of fascination and awe. Tales of a great flood that nearly wipes out all life are among humanity's oldest recorded stories, dating at least from the second millennium B.C., and they appear in cultures from the Middle East to the Arctic Circle to the southernmost tip of South America and the islands of Polynesia. Typically gods are at the center of these ancient disaster tales—which is perhaps not too surprising, given the fact that the tales originated during a time when human beings were at the mercy of natural forces they did not understand.

To a great extent, we still are at the mercy of nature, as anyone who reads the newspapers or watches nightly news broadcasts can attest.

Hurricanes, earthquakes, tornados, wildfires, and floods continue to exact a heavy toll in suffering and death, despite our considerable knowledge of the workings of the physical world. If science has offered only limited protection from the consequences of natural disasters, it has in no way diminished our fascination with them. Perhaps that's because the scale and power of natural disasters force us as individuals to confront our relatively insignificant place in the physical world and remind us of the fragility and transience of our lives. Perhaps it's because we can imagine ourselves in the midst of dire circumstances and wonder how we would respond. Perhaps it's because disasters seem to bring out the best and worst instincts of humanity: altruism and selfishness, courage and cowardice, generosity and greed.

As one of the national chairmen of the American Red Cross, a humanitarian organization that provides relief for victims of disasters, I have had the privilege of seeing some of humanity's best instincts. I have witnessed communities pulling together in the face of trauma; I have seen thousands of people answer the call to help total strangers in their time of need.

Of course, helping victims after a tragedy is not the only way, or even the best way, to deal with disaster. In many cases planning and preparation can minimize damage and loss of life—or even avoid a disaster entirely. For, as history repeatedly shows, many disasters are caused not by nature but by human folly, shortsightedness, and unethical conduct. For example, when a land developer wanted to create a lake for his exclusive resort club in Pennsylvania's Allegheny Mountains in 1880, he ignored expert warnings and cut corners in reconstructing an earthen dam. On May 31, 1889, the dam gave way, unleashing 20 million tons of water on the towns below. The Johnstown Flood, the deadliest in American history, claimed more than 2,200 lives. Greed and negligence would figure prominently in the Triangle Shirtwaist Company fire in 1911. Deplorable conditions in the garment sweatshop, along with a failure to give any thought to the safety of workers, led to the tragic deaths of 146 persons. Technology outstripped wisdom only a year later, when the designers of the luxury liner *Titanic* smugly declared their state-of-the-art ship "unsinkable," seeing no need to provide lifeboat capacity for everyone onboard. On the night of April 14, 1912, more than 1,500 passengers and crew paid for this hubris with their lives after the ship collided with an iceberg and sank. But human catastrophes aren't always the unforeseen consequences of carelessness or folly. In the 1940s the leaders of Nazi Germany purposefully and systematically set out to exterminate all Jews, along with Gypsies, homosexuals, the mentally ill, and other so-called undesirables. More recently terrorists have targeted random members of society, blowing up airplanes and buildings in an effort to advance their political agendas.

The books in the GREAT DISASTERS: REFORMS AND RAMIFICATIONS series examine these and other famous disasters, natural and human made. They explain the causes of the disasters, describe in detail how events unfolded, and paint vivid portraits of the people caught up in dangerous circumstances. But these books are more than just accounts of what happened to whom and why. For they place the disasters in historical perspective, showing how people's attitudes and actions changed and detailing the steps society took in the wake of each calamity. And in the end, the most important lesson we can learn from any disaster—as well as the most fitting tribute to those who suffered and died—is how to avoid a repeat in the future.

Auto-da-Fé

The 16th-century Spanish town square is a seething mass of spectators. Hundreds, maybe thousands, of people stand elbow to elbow, jostling for the best view of the balconies and raised platforms, hoping to catch a glimpse of the king, queen, or other important dignitaries who will be attending. It is here where the grand inquisitor will stand, clothed in royal purple, presiding over all. And it is here where the formal sentencing will take place for the prisoners of the Holy Office of the Inquisition.

People have traveled great distances to witness what will be, for many, a once-in-a-lifetime event: the *auto-da-fé*, or "act of faith." This auto-da-fé will be a most impressive ceremony, filled with pomp and grandeur. Events of this magnitude are costly and rare. Townspeople and peasants alike—

whose lives are often filled with hard work, monotony, and relative isolation—flock to the square, drawn by the promise of entertainment and religious renewal. Prisoners who have long awaited sentencing have been gathered together from the surrounding districts and will finally hear their fate. The crowd hushes as the ceremony begins.

A long procession of church and state officials, prisoners, and guards slowly winds its way from the cathedral to the square. Spectators crane their necks to see the unusual objects carried in the procession; beautiful, ornate golden crucifixes and rich, colorful banners sweep past. Torches and loads of wooden fuel also go by, conveyed to the appropriate areas. Muddy, reeking coffins, other wooden boxes with flames painted on the sides, and life-sized pasteboard images of absent prisoners lend a chilling and macabre air to the scene.

Some of these pasteboard images, or effigies, represent missing prisoners who have hidden or fled the country. These fugitives will be the first condemned because, in the minds of the officials, running away implies guilt. Their lands will be taken and their family members will be treated as second-class citizens.

The other effigies represent prisoners who have "escaped" by dying before this auto-da-fé. Some have died of disease or other natural causes while spending months, years, or even decades in prison awaiting their sentencing. Others have succumbed to the effects of the torture that was used to extract their confessions. No matter. The dead have only delayed sentencing—not escaped it. Inside the reeking coffins and boxes are their remains, dug up and brought to the auto-da-fé for burning. The officials of the Inquisition have made sure that everyone who deserves sentencing is present.

The hordes of onlookers force their eyes away from the grisly boxes and seek a new curiosity—the live prisoners.

The prisoners are easy to identify. In separate groups of men and women they trudge, ropes around their necks, each carrying a torch and accompanied by two or more church officials, called *familiares*. The prisoners walk barefoot, some wailing and weeping, some stone silent. Most of them wear garments of shame: three-foot-tall pointed hats, and sleeveless robes called *sanbenitos*. Most of the sanbenitos are yellow, with diagonal red crosses on the front and back. But two of the prisoners are wearing black robes adorned with painted flames, devils, and monsters. They were notified of their fates yesterday to give them time to prepare their souls. They are the ones condemned to death at the stake.

The prisoners are by far the most interesting part of the procession, being recognizable members of the community. Criminals, public nuisances, friends, neighbors, family members—even high-level officials— can be found in the group of prisoners. The richest man in town shuffles by in his yellow sanbenito. Many recall how he used to strut around in his fine clothes, and some no doubt feel a slight sense of satisfaction in seeing his public humiliation. But the procession is long and slow, and the spectators begin to grow impatient for the next part of the auto-da-fé, the Mass. The prisoners are led to their holding area on the left side of the raised platform, and the Mass begins.

This Mass is a solemn ceremony designed to renew the people's relationship with God. During the Mass, a church official gives a sermon, during which he reminds everyone of the specific articles of their Roman Catholic faith and clarifies the concept of sin. Church leaders then urge spectators and prisoners alike to examine their consciences and to repent of their sins. Renewed in their faith, the onlookers now turn their attention to the next phase of the ceremony, the sentencing.

An inquisitor announces prisoners' sentences. The grand spectacle of the auto-da-fé was designed to both inspire awe and renew religious faith.

First comes the roll call. As the accused answer to their names, they are led, one at a time, up to the platform to hear their sentence. The crowd is abuzz. The condemned are caged, standing on display in shame and humiliation so that all will see and remember.

Once again, the spectators gawk at the prisoners' varied expressions. A few of the faces seem hewn from granite, their features showing nothing save, perhaps, a steely determination. With others, however, the eyes betray a storm of emotions: eyes that blaze in defiance and anger; wide-open eyes shifting wildly in terror; hopeless, vacant eyes staring blankly in resignation or madness. Someone begins intoning the sentences, and dramatic reactions sweep through the crowd.

Even the stone-faced prisoners now show the strain of the moment. One lucky prisoner crumples in relief when he hears that his case has been dismissed. A few prisoners show relief tempered with what appears to be a vague apprehension when they hear that their cases have been suspended. While this means that they are free for now, if any new evidence is uncovered in the future, the officials of the Inquisition may come for them again in the dark of night and their ordeal will resume. A buzz of surprise sweeps through the crowd when the next prisoner is found innocent and actually acquitted—a rarity at an auto-da-fé.

Much more common are the convictions, along with appropriate penances, or punishments, which are declared next. Prisoners who have voiced sorrow for their sins and proclaimed their willingness to accept their punishments have saved themselves from the stake. Once their punishments have been carried out, they will be welcomed back into the Church. From now on they must always be on their best behavior, however, for any relapse, or return to sin, will result in death at the stake.

Milder punishments require a combination of prayers, public service, and fasting. Some of the accused hear that they will be stripped to the waist and ridden through town while receiving 100 to 200 lashes with a whip. One of them, an old woman, falls to her knees upon hearing this sentence. Others are sentenced to "perpetual" prison, which may mean anything from house arrest for a few months to lifelong incarceration. A prisoner faints when he hears that he is sentenced to undertake a pilgrimage to the Holy Land, for everyone present knows

Examples of sanbenitos. This page: Costumes of impenitent or relapsed offenders condemned to death. Opposite page: Costumes of individuals who confessed to the Inquisition. Though spared execution, such people were required to wear their sanbenitos in public for the rest of their lives.

that these religious journeys are dangerous and grueling. His wife and children begin weeping, fearing that they may never see him again. Another prisoner, a known troublemaker, is sentenced to the galleys; for five years he'll be a rower on board one of His Majesty's ships. Many prisoners are stunned to hear that their penance will involve the confiscation of some or all of their land and property. Though they have escaped the death penalty, the Inquisition has condemned them and their families to a life of begging in the streets.

One of the most severe penalties is banishment, or exile. Two prisoners receive this sentence and will now be forced to leave their homes and loved ones for many years. The enduring punishment of the sanbenito will affect a far greater number of people, both guilty and innocent, than any of the other penances. The sanbenito is an outward sign of guilt and shame, and those who have been sentenced in this way must wear the garment whenever they are in public. They will live in humiliation, marked as outcasts. Their families will face contempt and suspicion for many years to come. Death itself cannot erase the stain, for upon the death of the convicted, his or

her personal sanbenito, complete with name and sin, will be hung in the local church. Sanbenitos that decay with age and fall apart will be replaced with new ones bearing the same names, for the Inquisition requires them to remain as a perpetual reminder for all future generations.

Church officials, satisfied that so many sinners have been brought back to the faith, now turn to the business of the unrepentant. Church law forbids the Church's involvement in bloodshed in the name of the faith, so the inquisitors proclaim the names of the *relajados,* or those who are now handed over to the secular (civil or nonreligious) branch of government for sentencing. Secular officials call out the sentence of the doomed— death by fire.

Sentences having finally been given, the king is presented with a ceremonial token, a tiny bundle of kindling tied with ribbon to add to the execution fires. The condemned are mounted on mules and ridden to the place of execution, the *quemadero,* or "burning place." The *quemadero* is ready for its victims. Mounted there are a white cross and two wooden stakes, one for each of the condemned.

A mound of firewood is piled at the base of each stake. Green wood, which burns slowly, is reserved for the worse of the two criminals. The dry wood will be used for the man who was deemed worthy of a swifter and less painful death.

The condemned are led to the stake and bound to it with ropes around their ankles, knees, thighs, waist, chest, and neck. A lighted torch is passed before their eyes to remind them of the fate that awaits their doomed souls. They are given one last chance; priests bring crucifixes close to the prisoners' lips, imploring them to embrace their faith by kissing the cross, thereby saving their souls from eternal fire.

A kneeling priest suddenly bolts to his feet and tenderly embraces one of the condemned. The executioner standing behind the stake comes forward and hugs the prisoner. The news sweeps through the crowd like wildfire—one of the criminals has kissed the crucifix. The religious are joyous that a soul has been saved. Prayers are offered to a God who, in His infinite mercy, has allowed a door of heaven to be opened to the condemned.

However, the condemned man's kiss has bought for him not physical salvation, but a "merciful" death. New orders are whispered to the executioner, who nods his head. He steps behind his victim and swiftly strangles him to death just before the fire is lit.

Moments later the stench of burning flesh fills the air.

■   ■   ■

This nightmarish scene of an auto-da-fé actually happened as part of the ceremony of the Holy Office of the Inquisition. Scenes just like it, in fact, were repeated again and again during the course of more than 350 years of Spanish history.

Tolerance is a fairly recent concept, and Europe experienced many centuries of persecution and bloodshed. Criminals, troublemakers, people with mental illness, and freethinkers were considered dangerous and typically faced harsh punishments, including public execution.

Many people the world over have heard of the notorious Spanish Inquisition, but many are unaware that the horrors of the Inquisition were not limited to Spain. Kingdoms across the European continent—many in present-day Germany, Italy, and France—conducted their own ghastly versions of the Inquisition. The infamous Spanish Inquisition, however, is perhaps better known because of its far-reaching grasp: it stretched its tentacles clear across the Atlantic Ocean, putting a choke-hold on hapless victims in the New World as well. One of the most well known incidents of the Inquisition in the New World is the tragic story of the Carvajal family.

Admiral Luis de Carvajal y de la Cueva, known as the great conquistador, brought his family to the New World around 1580. He arrived at the port of Tampico, Mexico, with his wife, sister, brother-in-law, and their children. The New World offered them hope for a better life. Unfortunately, in 1584, Luis's brother-in-law died, leaving a wife and nine children. Luis took his sister Francisca and her large brood under his protection. Lacking children of his own, Luis named one of her sons, Luis *"el mozo"*—which means "the younger"— his heir. Together they explored the northern reaches of Spain's Mexican territory, traveling almost to the present-day Texas border. During that time, young Luis had a secret so dark that he couldn't even share it with his uncle, who first became aware of the trouble when officials of the Inquisition arrested him.

Luis's niece, Isabel, had caught the attention of the authorities by carelessly committing what to the Inquisition was an unforgivable sin: "Judaizing." Judaizers were people who had been baptized and pretended to be Catholics, but who were, in fact, practicing Jews. In 1589 Isabel and the rest of her family were taken into custody for questioning. Under torture, someone in the family started naming names. Eventually, Isabel's mother, sisters, and brothers—even her dead father—had been named as conspirators. Almost every living relative of the Carvajal family was arrested and thrown into jail. Not even Uncle Luis—who by now carried the title of "Governor of the New Kingdom of León"—was spared. He too was arrested and jailed for prolonged questioning about his involvement in his family's crime.

Luis *el mozo* was kept in a jail cell close to his mother's cell. From there he heard her agonized screams as inquisitors inflicted a horrible torture: binding and stretching on the rack.

While in jail, Luis began to have visions in his dreams. These visions gave him guidance and spiritual strength. He changed his name to Joseph, the Enlightened, and became the spiritual leader of his family, guiding them through their ordeals. Their troubles, the Carvajal family soon realized, were just beginning.

Months of prison and torture culminated in the auto-da-fé of February 24, 1590, when the entire Carvajal family was found guilty—including Francisco, Francisca's dead husband. His remains were dug up and burned, but the rest of the family saved themselves by repenting. The Church proclaimed their penances, welcomed them back to the faith, and warned them of the dangers of relapsing into sin. The family was sentenced to work in hospitals and convents without pay. For years

Officers of the Spanish Inquisition attempt to wring a confession from Isabel de Carvajal. Torture was a commonly accepted practice of the Inquisition, as it was with secular authorities during the Middle Ages.

afterward, the Carvajal family never felt safe. The Inquisition was always watching them—watching and waiting for another chance to pounce.

Five years later the Inquisition struck again. Somewhere, in a dark torture chamber, someone they knew had denounced them. The Carvajals were jailed and tortured for almost two years before the next *auto* sealed their fate.

In a grand auto-da-fé in Mexico City on December 8, 1596, Luis *el mozo,* his mother Francisca, and three of his sisters—Isabel, Leonor, and Catalina—were burned at the stake. Another sister, Mariana, was declared insane, but less than five years later, during the *auto* of 1601, she too was burned at the stake. The Inquisition allowed the youngest sister, Ana, to live, judging her too young to be executed. Another family raised her until she grew up, married another secret Jew, and had a family of her own. Eventually the Inquisition caught up to Ana as well; she died in prison in 1647. Her bones were later dug up and burned in an *auto* in 1649.

Governor Luis de Carvajal, in spite of his high position, faced a painful fate as well. Stripped of his land and title and sentenced to six years of exile from New Spain, he was sent back to prison to await departure for Spain. Four months later he died in prison of unknown causes. Of the entire Carvajal family, only two brothers, Miguel and Baltazar, escaped the Inquisition.

The Carvajals weren't the only people sentenced at the famous auto-da-fé of December 8, 1596. That day, the Inquisition imposed penances on many offenders, for crimes ranging from lying to murder. However, the Inquisition reserved its fullest fury for the most dangerous offenders of all—those found guilty of heresy, or error against their religion. Heretics who either refused to abandon their dangerous ideas or "relapsed" after having been pardoned could not be allowed to threaten the safety of everyone else. The only way to deal with them was to remove them from society—permanently.

Historians believe that tens of thousands of people were questioned by the Spanish Inquisition. Modern scholars estimate that about 2 percent of those questioned were condemned as heretics and burned alive. A little-known, but important, fact, however, is that Spain was neither the first nor the worst in her treatment of heretics. Many kingdoms, having battled heresy for centuries, set a grisly example for Spain to follow.

A medieval illuminated manuscript depicts Jews, with their characteristic peaked caps, tying Jesus to the cross. Many Christians of the Middle Ages blamed Jews for the death of Christ —a factor that contributed to the bloodletting that would occur during the Spanish Inquisition.

Laying the Kindling

T he roots of the Inquisition extend far back in time, to some of the earliest years of recorded history. The early history of Europe is a story of struggle, of continuous conquest and reconquest. People settled promising regions and established prosperous communities, only to be invaded by others who wanted the same land. This pattern continued for many centuries, with smaller, weaker civilizations falling to stronger or more ruthless newcomers.

In rare instances, conquering armies may have shown tolerance toward the conquered people, allowing them to retain their customs and beliefs. However, it was customary to massacre the entire population, to run them off, or to enslave them. After all, the conquered people represented a continual threat to the newcomers.

The Romans, a strong military power in ancient times, developed a new way to deal with the conquered. Romans often allowed their subjects to retain some autonomy for a time, giving these people the status of partial Roman citizenship. Both cultures coexisted, with the Romans enjoying the greater benefits that came with full citizenship. Over time, the conquered people were elevated to the status of full citizens. In this manner, Rome stretched the boundaries of its territory to become, by way of vast expansion throughout the Mediterranean region, the mighty Roman Empire.

In spite of the Romans' policy of tolerating the customs of vanquished peoples, however, clashes between the conquerors and the conquered frequently erupted. Such was the situation when the Roman Empire gained control of the Middle East and encountered the Jews.

For millennia, the Jewish people had been held together by their religion. The world's first monotheists (people who believe in the existence of a single God), the Jews had throughout their history suffered defeat and oppression at the hands of pagan cultures. In the first century B.C., the Romans became the latest in the long line of conquerors when their armies swept through Palestine.

The Jews had always believed that they were God's chosen people, and their scriptures predicted that God would send a Messiah, or savior, to deliver them. When Jesus of Nazareth, a child of Jewish parents, began preaching and reportedly performing miracles in their midst, some Jews began to wonder whether he might be their long-anticipated savior.

After his teachings angered Jewish leaders and drew the attention of the Roman governor of Palestine, however, Jesus was executed by crucifixion. But his death on the cross did not diminish Jesus' influence. Followers came to believe that Jesus had been sent by God not to deliver the Jews from political and military oppression, but, through his death, to redeem sinful humanity. Many people originally of the Jewish faith became followers of Jesus Christ (literally, "the Anointed") and began calling themselves Christians. Others who had never been Jewish joined the ranks of Christians.

Rome tried to combat the spread of Judaism and Christianity by enacting laws requiring people to worship Rome's pagan gods and by imposing severe penalties for failure to do so. Jews and Christians, taught that it was a sin to worship any but the "one, true God," refused to comply.

Though the Romans wanted to suppress both Judaism and Christianity, they perceived Christianity as a much bigger threat. This newcomer religion was gaining followers at an alarming rate, and Rome responded by ferociously persecuting Christians. One appalling practice was to throw Christians to hungry wild animals, a popular spectator sport among the residents of Rome.

In spite of this persecution, Christianity continued to spread until there were two powerful monotheistic religions in the world, Judaism and Christianity. Around A.D. 312–313, the Roman emperor Constantine converted to Christianity. Soon he issued an edict mandating tolerance for the religion, and eventually Christianity became the official religion of the entire Roman Empire. Because the center of the Church was Rome, and because Christianity thus spread throughout the vast Roman Empire, the religion came to be called Roman Catholicism, the word *catholic* meaning "general" or "universal."

Three hundred years after Constantine's conversion, a third major monotheistic religion sprang up. This one traced its origins to an Arab merchant and prophet named Muhammad. Born in the Arabian Peninsula around 570, Muhammad acquired a reputation for honesty and fairness. After receiving what he called a series of revelations from the archangel Gabriel, Muhammad began preaching. He urged his people to abandon their corrupt ways and to be obedient to the will of Allah, or God. In spite of persecution and numerous military campaigns waged against him and his followers, Muhammad triumphed. He attracted a large following of believers called Muslims (or Moslems), whose new religion became known as Islam, which means submission (to God's will).

The Muslim armies gained a reputation for efficiency and ferocity, and by the time of Muhammad's death in 632, the entire Arabian Peninsula had come under the influence of Islam. In the century ahead, armies fighting under the banner of Islam would emerge from North Africa and invade Europe and the rest of the Middle East, thus bringing the three monotheistic religions into conflict. Despite many shared beliefs, adherents of these three powerful religions would, for hundreds of years thereafter, be locked in conflict.

By the time Islamic military power began to be felt in Europe in the early 700s, the Roman Empire had been defunct for more than two centuries. With the final collapse of Roman authority in 476, western Europe entered an era that later scholars would refer to as the Middle Ages, roughly defined as the thousand-year period between the 5th and 15th centuries. During this time, western Europe experienced continual turmoil. Squabbles between kingdoms and monarchs were frequent, and invasions by Germanic tribes and Vikings added to the chaos.

Muhammad receives a chapter of the Koran from the archangel Gabriel. His features are blank because of the traditional Muslim prohibition against depicting the Prophet's image.

Christianity was one of the few unifying influences in western Europe during the Middle Ages. Most people counted themselves as Roman Catholics, but theirs was a religion tinged with superstition. Among common people, formal education didn't exist, and even the most rudimentary scientific knowledge was unknown. At the same time, constant challenges threatened people's survival: disease, floods, droughts, pestilence, and other natural disasters, along with enemy invasions, visited with alarming frequency. Lacking explanations for the whims of fate and seeking control over their lives, people turned to God. They attributed all that befell them to God's will and believed that the fate of an entire village might depend on each individual's relationship with God.

Christianity also offered the prospect of a better existence—eternal happiness in heaven—after death. This spiritual comfort may have been most important for those at the bottom of the medieval socioeconomic scale—the serfs, or peasants.

In many respects, serfs—the largest group of people— formed the backbone of feudalism, the economic and political system that dominated Europe during the early Middle Ages. Under the feudal system, social class was fixed by birth, and a serf's lot—indeed, his legal responsibility—was to cultivate a small plot of land owned by a nobleman, or lord. The serf owed a portion of the crops he grew, along with his loyalty, to the lord. In addition, the lord enjoyed near-total authority over his serfs; his will was essentially law. What the serfs received from this rather unequal relationship, in addition to being allowed to keep some of the crops they grew, was the lord's protection. With no education and no legal right to leave the land, serfs could look forward to a life of unceasing toil, beginning early in childhood and ending only with death.

By contrast, the comparatively small class of nobles, for whom the serfs labored, enjoyed significant privileges. They didn't need to perform backbreaking work because their lands generated wealth. Their male children received an education, were trained in the art of warfare, and might eventually become high-status knights. Their female children typically received instruction in the

domestic arts, in preparation for marriage. Yet nobles, like serfs, had responsibilities. The entire feudal system was based on allegiance, and lesser nobles promised their loyalty and service to more powerful nobles, who, in turn, owed their allegiance to the king.

The Catholic Church permeated all levels of feudal society, and it was much more than just a spiritual force. The Church implicitly sanctioned the feudal order and the vast inequalities associated with it. Indeed, the Catholic Church itself enjoyed great wealth, and evidence of this was plainly visible to everyone. Like children clustered around their mother's skirts, the dirty, unsanitary huts of the poor

This illuminated manuscript from the year 1300 shows a feudal lord giving orders to his serfs. Under the feudal system, serfs were legally bound to the land they cultivated.

surrounded magnificent, treasure-laden cathedrals in every town and village. Tithing—the requirement that everyone pay a tenth of his or her income to the Church—ensured a steady stream of revenue. The Church gave back in return: it cared for body and soul, shepherded the people in matters of faith, settled disputes, and provided food, shelter, and care for the poor.

In addition to its vast wealth, the Catholic Church wielded significant political influence during the Middle Ages. The relationship between church and state, or religion and government, was complicated, and determining just where civil power ended and church power began could be difficult. Popes expected secular rulers to yield to them in all spiritual matters and to support the Church's authority in their kingdoms. In return, the Church gave legitimacy to kings and queens. At coronation ceremonies, popes sometimes personally placed the crown on the head of the new monarch. This act symbolized the concept of the "divine right of kings," the idea that the new ruler governed with authority placed in him by God. Popes also mediated disputes between rival monarchs.

At times, however, conflict arose between secular and religious leaders. Monarchs sometimes believed—justifiably, in many cases—that any expansion of Church authority would come at their expense. Still, throughout most of the Middle Ages, the Roman Catholic Church and western Europe's secular rulers remained closely allied. Few people questioned the Church's authority, and those who did put themselves at great risk.

Over time, the Church itself became highly hierarchical. At the head of the religious hierarchy stood the pope in Rome, and in theory all church officials—cardinals, bishops, priests, and nuns—answered to him. With few exceptions, the clergy were selected from the ranks of the literate nobility. Many held deep religious convictions, but some were appointed because of their political connections or their ability to read and write.

Each bishop was placed in charge of a district, or diocese, and was expected to visit all the individual parishes (local church communities) in that diocese. This often involved dangerous and uncomfortable travel. Priests, on the other hand, typically served the people of a single parish.

Monks and friars formed a separate branch of the clergy. They tended to be well educated and strictly religious. Living apart from society in monasteries, they grew their own food, copied religious documents by hand, sometimes traveled the countryside to teach, and lived simple lives of devotion to God. Their monasteries grew into centers of learning, often becoming the foundation for later colleges and universities.

Church officials were expected to model the life of Jesus Christ by practicing celibacy (a life of abstinence from sexual relations), by preaching, and often by renouncing all but the most basic of life's necessities. Some of them succeeded in this difficult goal and lived model lives of service. Others, however, did not.

The religious life placed a huge burden on those who embraced it. Some people entered these positions with high intentions. Their chosen lifestyle was a continual struggle against human nature, for they rejected the "pleasures of the flesh." This meant avoiding sexual relations, eating and drinking only the sparest of meals, spending long hours in prayer, and working tirelessly in the service of God.

For others, though, there was never a struggle in the first place. These men sought the priesthood for selfish motives. The lures of easy work, easy money, and the potential for self-advancement were powerful incentives.

With its volatile mix of the pious, the weak, and the dishonest, the integrity of the Church began to suffer. Soon the smell of corruption began to foul the air. Some bishops and priests, finding the rigorous demands of their office too taxing, gave in to temptation and pursued lives of idleness and luxury. With increasing anger, people began to understand that the overburdened backs of the peasants supported the clergy's self-indulgent lifestyles. In addition, despite their vows of celibacy, some clergy-men gained unsavory reputations for keeping girlfriends or soliciting sex from churchgoers in exchange for forgiveness of sins.

Common church practices such as simony and the selling of indulgences caused further resentment. Simony was the act of buying a post within the Church. For the right price the well-to-do could buy their way into a high position such as bishop or archbishop. This often resulted in the shirking of duties, one of which was to visit the people within the diocese. Some corrupt clergymen spent more time visiting rich friends or hunting than tending to their flock of believers. Gail B. Stewart cites one example of this misuse of power in her book *Life During the Spanish Inquisition*. She tells of Archbishop Berenger, who "thirteen years after his [buying the office] had not yet visited his diocese [official territory]."

The business of selling indulgences became another common misuse of Church authority. In this practice, the church absolved, or forgave, sins in exchange for money—abandoning the traditional Catholic teaching that sins would be forgiven only through genuine repentance. Some of the poorest peasants scrimped and saved for long periods of time, even going without food in order to save enough money to buy indulgences. People placed great value in having their sins forgiven,

for they believed that if they died with the taint of sin they would be doomed to hell for all eternity.

Corruption was especially widespread in the south of France. In increasing numbers, common people began to feel neglected and bitter. In place of their former trust, obedience, and devotion, many began to view the Church and its clergy with increasing mistrust, suspicion, and contempt. Seeing a need for reform, some of the dissatisfied split from the Roman Catholic Church to form new religious groups of their own. The Church, feeling threatened by this challenge, labeled the growing trend "heresy" and moved to stamp it out.

An ornate, gold-leaf indulgence box into which the faithful could put money in exchange for forgiveness of their sins. Corrupt practices such as the selling of indulgences inspired some groups to break with the Catholic Church—which in turn contributed to the Church's decision to launch the Inquisition.

Heresy Creates Sparks

3

eresy is defined as an error in faith, and that's exactly what the Church felt was being committed by people who left Catholicism to form new religious groups. In the Middle Ages heresy was considered not simply a crime against God, but also a crime against society. Those who erred simply needed education to turn them back to the true faith. However, those who knowingly persisted in their errors were heretics, and they were treated as criminals. In fact, heretics were considered worse than murderers, since heretics murdered the soul.

The occasional heretic posed little threat to the Church, so for the most part, the Church rarely concerned itself with isolated individuals who weren't attracting followers. Besides, townspeople usually squelched heretical thinkers quickly for fear that they might create a major problem.

...ɣ to Albert C. Shannon, author of *The Medieval* ... common people considered heretics so ...hat the first violent reactions came not from ...s, ecclesiastical or civil, but from the ...lves." Such was the fate of Peter of Bruys.

...nonk who left his monastery sometime in ... 1100s to preach against the Roman Catholic ...urch. He especially disapproved of the reverence shown toward the cross. One day, while he was burning a stack of crosses, an irate mob seized him and threw him into the same fire that he had lit.

In the religious climate of Europe's Middle Ages, distinction was not made between heretical thinking and the commission of a crime. People who rejected Church law denied civil law and, in effect, declared themselves outlaws. And criminals of all types faced harsh consequences.

To modern sensibilities, medieval punishments seem disproportionately severe. A person found guilty of stealing, for example, might have a finger or a hand cut off. Other common punishments included branding with a hot iron, whipping, mutilation, and death by beheading, disemboweling, or burning alive. Even the milder punishments left the offender a marked criminal for the rest of his or her life.

To make matters worse, medieval Europe lacked a rational system for judging guilt and innocence. Authorities established the truth through methods such as trial by combat or trial by ordeal. In a trial by combat, the accuser and the accused battled to the death. God, it was believed, would come to the aid of the person telling the truth, so the victor in the combat was judged to have proved his case.

The trial by ordeal usually involved either the hot or cold method. The hot method required the accused to grasp a red-hot object such as an iron bar or to plunge his

...ainting by the Spanish
...dro Berruguete
...int Dominic
...he burning of
...oks. Efforts
...Albigensian
...e foun-
...tion.

The varieties of medieval punishment. Though the methods of the Inquisition were brutal, they were the same ones employed by the secular authorities of the time.

or her hand into boiling water. The burns were bandaged for three days, then inspected for signs of infection. If infection was present, the accused was judged guilty. In the cold water ordeal, the accused was bound and thrown into a body of water that had been blessed. If the accused person floated, he or she was found guilty (and frequently then executed), for it was believed that God's presence in the water had rejected the person. (An "innocent" defendant, whom God had accepted into the water, might drown.)

After being officially forbidden by Pope Innocent III in 1215, ordeals were abandoned as a means of determining guilt. Conviction, therefore, depended upon other means of proof—either the testimony of at least two eyewitnesses or, better still, the suspect's own confession. To extract such a confession authorities turned to a technique borrowed from the Roman Empire: the use of torture.

Court administrators began to use torture as a means of ascertaining guilt, whether or not the Church approved. They already had at their disposal a full array of tools, for human ingenuity had invented specialized devices designed to inflict pain and damage to every imaginable part of the body. Administrators could choose from devices that crushed bones, stretched ligaments, burnt and tore flesh, pierced organs, or dislocated joints. Sometimes just the sight of the horrific devices, embellished with ornate and gruesome etchings, was enough to wrench a confession from a stubborn tongue.

Medieval societies also began to make use of another legacy from the Roman Empire: Rome's code of law. Under this system, law cases began with a private accusation. A citizen who accused a neighbor of a crime was responsible for providing proof of those claims. Both accuser and accused agreed to abide by the decision of the person chosen to act as mediator. As a result of frivolous accusations, however, an amendment was soon added. The accuser now had to prove the case or face the same penalty that the accused would have met if the case had been proven.

This amendment, while stemming the tide of frivolous accusations, effectively discouraged citizens from reporting crime altogether. With the decrease in the number of accusations brought against wrongdoers, it may be assumed that crime increased. As a result, the mediator's role began to change. Instead of passively waiting for an accusation, he became responsible for actively seeking out and trying suspected lawbreakers. This was the system in place when the Church became concerned about rumors of heretics forming large communities throughout the Christian world.

Europe had seen minor heresies come and go for centuries. From time to time, individuals emerged to preach doctrines the Church considered erroneous. Typically, however, these heretics weren't well organized and didn't attract large followings. Oftentimes, heretical groups formed and flourished for a time, but declined after the passing of their leader. In northern France and Germany especially, the passing of a would-be heretical leader tended to be particularly rapid. In these regions, mobs were quick to rise up against suspected heretics, whom they seized and burned at the stake, often without benefit of a trial.

In the south of France by the end of the 12th century, however, a few heresies took root and flourished. One of the first groups to attract the Church's attention were the Waldensians, whose influence eventually spanned decades.

Their leader, Valdes, was a rich merchant of Lyons who came to believe that the way to heaven was to give away all of his possessions and to preach the word of God. After making arrangements for the care of his wife and child, he went out as a beggar to preach. Common people were impressed by his plain lifestyle, which contrasted sharply with the luxurious lifestyles of some Church officials.

Disgruntled and feeling abandoned by the Church, some of these poor and illiterate people began to follow Valdes. The Waldensians, or "Poor Men," as they came to be called, soon attracted the attention of the archbishop of Lyons, who forbade Valdes to preach. The archbishop's rationale was that people without proper training and approval could not be allowed to spread dangerous mistakes in the teaching of the faith.

Valdes continued to preach anyway, so the archbishop

expelled him from the city. His followers eventually broke into two groups. The Poor of Lyons remained in the south of France, and the Poor Lombards settled in northern Italy.

In comparison with other heretical groups, the Waldensians posed little real threat to the Church. Other than casting a bad light on corrupt bishops, the Waldensians remained essentially Catholic because their teachings were basically the same as those of the Church.

By contrast, the Albigensians held convictions that were in direct opposition to Church doctrine. Named after the Albi region of France where it first flourished, the Albigensian heresy grew to such alarming proportions that the pope himself was forced to take action against it. From the Church's point of view, what made the Albigensians—also known as Cathars, from the Greek word meaning "perfect"—especially dangerous, was their influence over great numbers of people and their ability to attract new members across generations. In addition, the Church considered their beliefs particularly deviant.

The Albigensians believed in two gods. The good god was the creator of the soul and all things good. The evil god created the human body and the material world, which were, therefore, evil. The Albigensians' goal was to free the good soul from the evil body so that it could return to its home in heaven. The soul could reside in human and animal bodies until it reached a state of perfection and went to heaven.

To the Albigensians, sexual relations were evil; therefore, marriage was also evil. By extension, pregnancy was evil, as were children, who came from pregnancy. Since the Albigensians believed that all sins were equal in seriousness, they believed that children would receive the same punishment in eternity as thieves and murderers.

The Albigensians were divided into two groups:

the "Credentes," or believers, and the "Perfects," or "perfected." The Credentes' only obligation was to receive the sacrament of the *consolamentum* before they died.

The *consolamentum* was a kind of confirmation, which transformed a person from a Credente into a Perfect. Once "perfected," a person had to abide by a set of stringent rules. Perfects had to practice absolute celibacy and avoid certain foods that were the by-products of sexual activity, such as meat, milk, eggs, and cheese. The perfected fasted three days a week and took part in three 40-day fasting periods every year. Only the Perfects were allowed to pray, and they wore black clothing as a sign of their status. As a result of later persecutions, however, the perfected replaced their distinct uniform with a hidden black thread sewn under their clothes.

Because of the difficult lifestyle of the perfected, many people delayed receiving the *consolamentum* for as long as possible, often waiting until they were near death. Death, however, was difficult to predict. If, after receiving the *consolamentum,* the sick person seemed to be making an unwelcome recovery, death could be hastened with the *endura,* a method used to kill a person by starvation. It was even used on children, who normally were not allowed to receive the *consolamentum.*

In spite of its radical ideas, Albigensianism had appeal. The Albigensians claimed that the Catholic Church was a false church, and that theirs was the only true religion. Furthermore, they promised heaven to all who received the *consolamentum.* In the meantime, Credentes were free to continue living as they always had; encouraged by the *consolamentum's* eventual promise of salvation, many felt free to live lives of sin and excess.

Albigensianism appealed to the uneducated; it attracted many followers and spread through the south of France. It was this rapid growth that so disturbed the

Church, which recognized a need for action toward the latter part of the 12th century.

Pope Innocent III saw three choices before him: education, reform, or repression. He started with education. Dominican and Franciscan monks were the chosen educators because their vows of poverty would give them credibility with common people, and their teaching skills were highly regarded.

Some Waldensians and Poor Lombards did voluntarily return to the warm welcome of the Church. Progress, however, was agonizingly slow and, in spite of the monks' efforts, heresy continued to grow and spread. It was obvious that something else had to be done, so the pope turned his attention to the corruption within the Church.

Innocent III cleaned house by dismissing approximately 10 bishops for simony, incompetence, negligence, or disobedience. He discovered, though, that not even education and reform were enough to halt the spread of the cancerous heresies. He soon recognized the need for some form of suppression, and over the last few decades of the 12th century a series of councils met to decide matters of policy. These councils would set in motion events that would have unforeseeable and far-reaching consequences.

The Council of Tours met in 1163 and drafted a document that condemned heresy and asked local clergy to seek out heretics and restore them to their senses. This was significant because it was the first official document that instructed clerics to take an active role in the suppression of heresy, rather than passively waiting for the customary accusation. Though it was mostly ignored, the document may have been the seed that germinated to become the Inquisition.

Later councils drafted documents calling for stricter measures against heresy. One such document denounced

Pope Innocent III confirms the order of Saint Francis. Innocent erroneously believed that heresy could be eliminated through the teaching efforts of Franciscan and Dominican monks.

those who "practice their wickedness no longer in secret . . . but preach their error publicly and thus mislead the simple and the weak." Secular officials were instructed to swear under oath to support the bishops and their special assistants, who had to visit all communities in which heresy was suspected. In addition, the councils decided on a formal definition. Heretics were defined as those who preached without permission, whose teachings differed from those of the Roman Church, who were excommunicated by the local bishop for heresy, and who assisted or defended heretics. The final part of the definition was significant because it opened the door for heretics and their supporters to suffer the same consequences.

Heretics could always repent, swear sincerity, and return to the faith. Relapsed or unrepentant heretics would be excommunicated by the Church (which jeopardized one's chances for eternal salvation) and handed over to the secular arm for consequences such as exile or confiscation of property. This was justified by the fact that in Roman law confiscation was an accepted punishment for treason (betrayal of the allegiance owed to a ruler). Heresy would be treated the same because it represented treason against the supreme ruler, God. Relapsed heretics were declared "infamous," which barred them from clerical and secular office and prevented them from giving testimony.

Despite the strict nature of these measures, they were intended more as a means of persuasion than of punishment. The pope's intent was to care for the souls entrusted to him, and he sincerely hoped that these measures would persuade heretics to return to the true faith.

Ultimately, however, a half-century of efforts against heresy ended in failure. In spite of educational efforts, reforms, and official decrees, at the end of the 12th century Albigensianism was still spreading. This was due, in part, to corrupt nobles, secular rulers, and incompetent or lazy clergymen.

In 1208, the murder of one of the pope's representatives by an unknown knight was the final blow. It convinced Innocent III of the need for a crusade, or holy war, against the heresies.

Responding to the pope's call to arms, about 500 troops from northern France gathered in 1209 to launch the first organized military campaign against heresy. More of a land grab by greedy nobles than an attempt to eliminate heresy, the Albigensian Crusade had earned a reputation for brutality through the unrestrained massacre of innocent people and heretics alike by the time it ended 20 years later. It did, however, achieve moderate success. The Albigensian Crusade halted the rampant progress of Catharism, whose followers thereafter were reduced to relatively small and isolated pockets throughout Europe.

Heresy continued to require constant vigilance,

however, and the Dominican and Franciscan monks found their tasks extremely difficult. In carrying out their duties, monks risked expulsion, bodily injury, and even death because local officials resented the monks' intrusion into their territories. Monks were required to work closely with local bishops, whose hostility often led to bitter disagreements. Unresolved conflicts were frequently referred to the pope in Rome, who found himself flooded with cases to untangle. A universal system was needed. So, between the years 1231 and 1233, Pope Gregory IX set up the office of the Inquisition to investigate all heretical matters.

Turmoil and abuses continued on all sides, however. For example, in 1234, in the vicinity of Albi, stronghold of the Albigensians, crowds roughed up an inquisitor and were about to throw him into the Tarn River when a group of defenders rescued him.

Another story tells of the controversy surrounding the Dominican monk and inquisitor William Arnold. When he called some citizens of the town of Toulouse to appear before him, they refused. Backed by Count Raymond VII, they expelled the inquisitor and all other Dominicans from town. William Arnold retaliated by excommunicating the count and consuls of Toulouse, who wrote to the pope to lodge a complaint. The pope forgave the count and granted some of the town's requests by suspending Inquisition activities there for six months. The Dominicans, angry at their ill treatment and lack of support from the pope, went on a strike that lasted three years.

In 1242, hatred toward the Inquisition inspired the Cathars to hatch a plot against the inquisitors. One night, assassins entered the church where William Arnold and nine of his companions were praying and hacked them to death with axes. The assassins then hid in the town of Montsegur, a Cathar stronghold. Local bishops and royal troops laid siege to the town for more than a year. When the inhabitants finally surrendered, the king's soldiers burned the unrepentant heretics.

Lacking sufficient supervision, inquisitors committed atrocities of their own. In Germany, Conrad of Marburg was assassinated for his zealous burning of heretics; in France, Robert the Bougre burned 180 people in one year. When the pope learned of this, he sentenced Robert to life imprisonment.

In the meantime, heresies continued to develop. The Flagellants, a traveling religious group that began in Italy and wandered into Germany, Hungary, Flanders, and Holland, promised salvation to all who shared in their ritual: exactly 33 and a half days of scourging their own half-naked bodies with metal-tipped whips. In 1349 Pope Clement VI declared them heretics. Some experts today believe that the Flagellants probably contributed to the spread of disease through their travels and bloodletting.

Conflict, both religious and secular, was the common element of succeeding centuries, and the Inquisition was the universal method for dealing with it. Initially established for religious reasons, the Inquisition became useful for political purposes as well, and two of its best-known victims illustrate this duality of purpose. Joan of Arc was condemned for political reasons and burned alive in 1431. Mathematician and astronomer Galileo Galilei was punished for disobeying the Inquisition's order to stop his unorthodox teaching about the movement of the earth. He was sentenced to life imprisonment in 1632. The sentence was later reduced to house arrest, which Galileo endured until his death in 1642.

The Inquisition's list of targets grew over the centuries to include not only heretics, but also political enemies and witches. The medieval Inquisition was so successful in its purpose of protecting the unity of the Church that other

The Flagellants, a traveling religious group that originated in Italy, taught that salvation could be won through a prescribed period of self-scourging. In 1349 Pope Clement VI declared the group's teachings heretical.

countries in western Europe, including Spain and Portugal, adopted its methods.

The medieval Inquisition operated chiefly in the 13th century in France, Germany, and Italy. Toward the end of the 15th century, some 200 years later, Spain's monarchs officially established the Holy Office of the Inquisition in their country. The Spanish government needed help in solving some irksome problems, and in this powerful institution there was great promise indeed.

Wisps of Smoke

T he Iberian Peninsula (later divided into Spain and Portugal) had always been viewed as a prized jewel because of its rich natural resources and strategic location in the Mediterranean. As a result, it endured countless invasions by various peoples.

Two groups, the Basques and the Iberians, settled the peninsula before recorded history. Later, Celts mingled with the Iberians, forming a group called the Celtiberians. The Phoenicians established trade centers on the peninsula around 1100 B.C., and Greeks arrived around 550 B.C. In the third century B.C., the Carthaginians sailed across the Mediterranean from North Africa and conquered much of the Iberian Peninsula. After routing the Carthaginians, Rome ruled Iberia between about 200 B.C. and the fifth century A.D. Visigoths vanquished the Romans and ruled from the fifth to the eighth century.

Over the centuries, small groups also migrated to the peninsula. One such group was the Jews, whose origins in Iberia remain a mystery. While many historians trace the Jews' origins in Spain to the first century A.D., other scholars believe that a Jewish presence there may go as far back as the sixth century B.C. Though a relatively small minority, Jews in Spain constituted the largest Jewish community in the world outside of Jerusalem.

Each wave of immigrants brought its own set of customs and religious beliefs, which led to a vast mixing of cultures. It is here, in this boiling cauldron of cultures, that the fires of the future Inquisition first sent up their tiny wisps of smoke.

In a move to unite his kingdom, the Visigoth leader King Reccared converted to Christianity in 587 and issued a number of laws against non-Christians. By his decree Jews could not own Christian slaves or marry Christians.

Reccared's successor, Sisebut, took matters a step further. For reasons unknown—and contrary to the Christian teachings of his day—Sisebut issued a shocking proclamation in 613. Non-Christians would not be tolerated; anyone wanting to remain in Spain would have to embrace Catholicism. No one knows how many Jews were forced to convert, but after a century of oppression they still had not fully integrated into Christian society.

By the end of the seventh century, the ruling Visigoths suspected that Jews were conspiring against them. In 694 the Visigoths announced that some Jews had confessed to plotting with North African Muslims to overthrow them. While there is no existing evidence to support this—and any confessions were likely extracted through torture—it is not hard to imagine why Jews may have wished to see their oppressors' downfall. Conspiracy or no, a short time later the Muslims, or Moors, left Africa and sailed north toward the Spanish coastline.

In 711, the Moors stormed the coast. They met with weak resistance and quickly conquered the southern areas of Spain. Sweeping northward, they met with stronger resistance, but within the space of three years they had occupied almost the entire peninsula, with the exception of a small, mountainous area in the north. Inhabitants of this territory remained Catholic and never let go of their dream to drive the invaders out of Spain.

When the Moors reached the south of France, they were stopped in their tracks; otherwise, much of Europe might have fallen to their mighty armies. By the middle of the eighth century the Muslims were the undisputed sovereigns of the Iberian Peninsula.

In 722, however, Christians celebrated their first victory against the Moors. This event marked the start of the *Reconquista,* or reconquest of Spain by the Christians. From that point on, periodic battles shifted the line separating Muslim and Christian territories.

The remarkable speed and success of the Moors' conquest of Spain leads to intriguing theories. Perhaps Spain fell to the Muslims' superior military training. Maybe the Visigoths' defenses were weak because of corruption and in-fighting. In any case, it is possible that the Jews, heavily oppressed by the Visigoths, might have welcomed the Moors. A widely accepted story claims that when the Moors arrived at Toledo, the city's Jews threw open the gates to them. Welcome or not, the Muslims intended to stay and, despite repeated attempts to expel them, held onto Spain with clenched fists. For almost 800 years, parts of Spain would live under Muslim rule.

The Moors immediately began the task of governing their new kingdom. The most pressing question was how to deal with the conquered people, mostly Christians and some Jews. How could the three religions exist side by side? The Muslims turned to their holy book, the Koran, for answers. The Koran, however, had conflicting instructions. Some passages indicated that infidels (non-believers) were enemies of the faith and should be put to the sword. Other passages called for tolerance toward "people of the book." Jews and Christians, whose faith, like the Muslims', centered on the "one, true God" of each religion's holy book, were "people of the book." So some Muslim rulers decided to let them live. They were to be classed as *dhimmis*, or protected minorities. Though they would have second-class status, Jews and Christians would be tolerated. They could pursue occupations of their own choosing, live wherever they wished, and freely practice their own religion.

This was a remarkable decision—remarkable for its very existence in the midst of an intolerant era. Nevertheless, some Muslims believed more strongly in the Koran's other message, and sporadic violence against the minorities erupted over the centuries. For example, after Yehosef ibn Nagrela, a Jewish vizier (adviser) in the Islamic court of Granada, fell out of favor and was murdered, a pogrom (organized killing) broke out in Granada's Jewish quarter. Rioting Muslims massacred 300 Jews and destroyed the entire community.

In spite of this simmering hostility, Muslim royals filled their courts with intelligent, learned, and influential leaders of the Jewish and Christian religious communities. These leaders were valuable to their overlords not only for their skills and training, but also for their influence with their own religious communities. For the most part, Jewish people felt relieved to be free of their Visigoth persecutors and adapted quickly to their new rulers.

A majority of Christians, however, resented their demotion to second-class status. They also felt an uncomfortable new emotion in regard to the Jews: envy. Jews were beginning to fill influential positions once held only by Christians.

Muslim royalty in need of translators increasingly turned to Jews. Their Hebrew language was close to Arabic, so they had a linguistic advantage over the Christians, with their Latin-based tongue. In addition, Jewish skill in medicine was widely recognized, so many royal households now employed the services of Jewish doctors. Furthermore, the Muslims preferred Jews for their skill in financial matters.

The favor enjoyed by these influential Jews began to extend beyond palace walls. The entire Jewish community in Moorish Spain began to flourish.

Despite the conflicts, Spain prospered under the influence of its enlightened lords during the 9th, 10th, and 11th centuries. To their capital city of Córdoba, Islamic rulers welcomed musicians, scientists, doctors, philosophers, artists, poets, and scholars. Education and culture flourished throughout the peninsula. Moorish accomplishments spurred Christians and Jews to artistic and intellectual achievements of their own.

During Islam's nearly 800 years of occupation, Spain eventually settled into a state of *convivencia,* or coexistence. For many people, even religious purity lost its former luster. Over time, a confusing stew of faith combinations emerged. Jews, Christians, and Muslims borrowed foreign customs, intermarried, and sometimes converted to another faith. This coexistence, however, was not always harmonious. For example, the Muslims' anti-Jewish feelings erupted from time to time in violent pogroms of entire Jewish communities. *Convivencia,* then, was like a deep river whose smooth surface hides the turbulent currents beneath.

Meanwhile, political forces were at work chipping away at the foundation of the Muslim kingdom. In the

Interior of the Great Mosque, Córdoba, Spain. The Moors presided over a flourishing of culture, and for the most part their rule was characterized by religious tolerance.

11th century Moorish Spain broke into 20 *taifas* (smaller kingdoms) as a result of internal conflict. These *taifas* weakened Muslim rule further by warring against one another. Also, the Christians in the north continued to win military victories. The Moors were being squeezed out, their domain shrinking as the northern border of their territory crept slowly southward.

By the 12th century Christians were beginning to feel a renewed sense of identity as they reestablished themselves as the dominant group. Somewhere between the relative tranquility of *convivencia* and the violent conflicts of the *Reconquista,* however, some Christians began to see the Jews as the source of all their troubles. Jews were already suspected of aiding the Muslim conquest. Furthermore, they appeared to have benefited from Muslim rule more than anyone else; Jews held some of the highest positions in the land.

For their part, the Jews sometimes unknowingly invited their neighbors' ill will, for they seemed to hold themselves apart from the rest of society. Believing themselves God's "chosen people," they often relished their separateness. Jews tended to live in enclaves; and though they lived in the country as well as in towns and villages, the stereotype was that they were rich town dwellers. It is easy to imagine why. Minorities who have things in common tend to gather together for companionship and community spirit. In times of persecution, grouping together offers an added benefit: safety.

Jewish communities tended to develop in towns because Jews often excelled at trades best suited to such an environment. Though educated Christians also lived in towns, Christians formed the bulk of the agricultural trade; they tended to live and work outside town as poor laborers and farmers. The concentration of wealthy Jewish doctors, scholars, merchants, tax collectors, and bankers in towns, therefore, caused jealousy among the poor common folk. They imagined that the Jews were unfairly controlling Spain's wealth.

Furthermore, Jewish people tended to avoid eating their meals with outsiders. Many Christians interpreted this as a sign of Jews' disdain for them. What they did not understand was the religious importance Jews attached to food and meals. For example, eating pork was forbidden; and old Jewish laws mandated many other strict guidelines regarding food selection and preparation, as well as mealtime ceremony.

Amid the *convivencia* of the mid-13th century, educated members of the elite upper class celebrated their differences. King Alfonso X, nicknamed "the Learned," proudly called himself the "king of the three religions" and ordered the translation of each religion's holy book into Spanish. However, the larger lower class didn't share this enlightened attitude. Disgruntled Christians accused Jewish merchants of unfair business practices. They believed that Jews favored their Jewish customers by offering them better products and lower fees. Smoldering hostilities and idle gossip combined to spawn vicious rumors. Jewish tax collectors were said to be siphoning off some of the people's money before sending the rest of it along to the royal treasuries. The rumors grew in ferocity and began to reflect a growing sense of paranoia among Christians.

Wild stories claimed that Jews were plotting to destroy Christianity. One tale accused Jews of tainting the wells used by Christians. Another said that Jewish doctors hid poison under their fingernails with which to kill their Christian patients. Strange tales of Jews practicing the dark arts—using the blood of tortured animals in their magic potions, or capturing Christian children and drinking their blood—frightened and enraged the Christians. The incredible tales swept from town to town.

In more enlightened times, these malicious rumors might have quickly died out. In the fertile soil of the Middle Ages, however, they grew like thorny vines—digging deep roots and sending spiny offshoots to choke out the flower of tolerance.

In the 1330s people began hearing strange and

frightening tales of a mysterious plague sweeping the Far East. It reportedly spread like wildfire and killed with astonishing ruthlessness. The rumored death totals were so staggering that they were hard to believe. Before long, however, the epidemic—called the Black Death— reached Spain and began to surge across the Iberian Peninsula. The year was 1348.

The Black Death, or what is today commonly known as bubonic plague, was a dreadful disease. People who contracted the illness first suffered with high fevers and vomiting. A short time later, swelling appeared in the lymph glands of the neck, armpits, and groin. These

Alfonso X, a 13th-century Spanish king, encouraged harmony between Christians, Jews, and Muslims. The illustration here, from a book Alfonso commissioned, shows Christians (at left) and Jews socializing. In spite of the king's efforts, however, suspicion and rancor persisted among Spain's religious groups.

lumps quickly darkened from pools of blood lying just beneath the skin. The lumps, or "buboes," became infected and oozed blood and pus. The victims spat blood and smelled foul. Three or four days after becoming ill, most of the victims would be dead.

No one knew what caused this horrible illness. What was even more frightening was that no one knew how to stop it. People began to suspect that it was spread through personal contact, but they couldn't do anything to stop its rampage. Towns and cities were the hardest hit, with residents dying by the thousands. Entire villages were wiped out.

People died faster than graves could be dug, and the bodies piled up. Sometimes corpses rotted where they fell because fear of the disease kept people from going near them. Great pits were dug and the dead dumped into mass graves. Historians believe that the plague killed one-fourth to two-thirds of the entire population of Europe, up to 25 million people.

Eventually the Black Death itself died out, and in 1350 Pope Clement VI declared a jubilee year to celebrate the survival of humanity. The bubonic plague would return, however, in smaller outbreaks in 1360 and 1369, and thereafter sporadically into the 16th century. In its horrifying wake, the plague left people stunned, disoriented, and looking for answers.

One medieval writer blamed the Black Death on a special alignment of planets that had occurred in 1345. Some people believed that the plague had blown in on the south wind, so they had their houses built with windows only on the northern sides. Some viewed the Black Death as the handiwork of Satan, while others believed it to be the punishment of God upon a sinful world. This thinking gave rise to the traveling Flagellants, the religious zealots who whipped themselves bloody to atone for the

world's wickedness. Spectators caught the blood with rags and smeared it on their eyes, thinking it had the power to work miracles. The only thing it did was spread infection.

The theories that gained the most momentum, however, were those that blamed neither planets, nor winds, nor God, nor Satan, but fellow human beings. Not surprisingly, minorities were the groups most frequently targeted. The French blamed the English; the Germans blamed the Jews.

By the time the Black Death disappeared completely from Spain in the mid-14th century, the Moors had been driven out of all areas except the small southern stronghold of Granada. Thus, when Spaniards looked for minorities to blame for the Black Death, their sights fell on the Jews.

Burying the dead during the Black Death. The cause of the epidemic, which devastated Europe in the mid-1300s, remained a mystery, and in the hysterical atmosphere of the times, many people in Spain and elsewhere blamed the Jews.

Spaniards noted that the Christian community had been harder hit than the Jewish community. If true, this was probably the result of the Jews' stricter sanitary and dietary laws. But medieval ignorance led people to the wrong conclusions. Pogroms against Jews took place all over Europe, but they were particularly fierce in Germany and Spain.

In Germany, a Jewish doctor was caught with a suspicious-looking powder in his possession. Though it was probably medicine, under torture he "confessed" that a rabbi had given him the powder to poison Christian wells. Jews' houses were bricked up with the inhabitants still inside, or Jews were herded into buildings that were then burnt to the ground. Some Jewish people were forced into barrels that were then thrown into rivers.

In southern Spain, Jews again became the targets of malicious slander. One man with a particularly fierce grudge against the Jews was Ferrant Martínez. In his opinion, Jews were guilty of the most horrendous crime in history: the murder of Jesus Christ. From his pulpit in Seville, he spent 12 years preaching hatred of the "Christ-killers." Despite Jewish appeals to the archbishop of Seville and the archbishop's admonishment that he stop spreading the propaganda, Martínez persisted. In the summer of 1391, violent mobs stormed the Jewish quarter of Seville. From there the frenzy spread across the peninsula. Henry Kamen, author of *The Spanish Inquisition,* describes the destruction: "In Seville hundreds of Jews were murdered and the aljama [Jewish quarter] was destroyed. . . . In Valencia during July, some two hundred and fifty were murdered; in Barcelona during August, some four hundred. The major aljamas of Spain were wiped out." Though royal authorities denounced the excesses and sheltered and fed Jews, the destruction of the Jewish community was catastrophic. As Kamen reports, "Seville had around five hundred Jewish families prior to the riots; a half-century later it had only fifty."

In all the cities where massacres took place, the Jews were given a choice: baptism or death. Across centuries of persecution in places such as Spain, England, France, and Germany, Jews had faced the same gut-wrenching decision. Much of the time, the Jews had chosen death over the betrayal of their faith. In the carnage of Spain's widespread pogroms of 1391, however, many Jews accepted baptism. Thousands converted to Christianity, forming a new class in society—the *conversos,* or converts.

In the aftermath of the bloodshed, recently converted Jews began the task of rebuilding their lives, neighborhoods, and even their greatly diminished populations. Many of these converted "New Christians" found new opportunities. High positions in royal Christian courts that had been closed to Jews before were now open to them because of their new status as Christians.

If these *conversos* thought that accepting the Catholic faith had put an end to their troubles, however, they were mistaken. Their new status left them in a difficult position: they had ties to both Christian and Jewish communities, but the full loyalty and support of neither. As the *conversos* were about to find out, their troubles were just beginning.

From Flicker to Flame

5

T he conversion of so many Jewish souls to Christianity did nothing to ease religious tension, but merely served to add new problems. Though people did not know it then, they were about to find out that this large, artificially created religious group would have trouble fitting in everywhere. Instead of just three conflicting religious groups, now there were four; and when *conversos* were added to the already-boiling pot of religions, the mixture boiled over.

Some *conversos* never got over their resentment at being forced to become Christian. Though the law forbade them to return to their former faith, they openly defied the law by flaunting their loyalty to Judaism. They faithfully attended Jewish services and made regular donations of oil to their local synagogues. Others rebelled in more subtle ways, such as pretending to take part in all the rituals connected with Christianity while secretly practicing as many of their old Jewish customs as possible. For example, some *conversos* made a good appearance of taking their children to church to be baptized into Christianity. During baptism, the child was anointed with water and holy chrism, a mixture of oils and balsam. As soon as these *conversos* returned to the safety of their homes, however, they removed all traces of the oils in order to "erase" the baptism.

If at first most *conversos* regretted their conversion, over time many began to accept their new religion. They were not immune to the advantages their new status afforded them. Finally free from persecution, most *conversos* eventually embraced Christianity with full sincerity. As early as two or three generations later, their offspring were found to be devout Christians, completely integrated into Christian society.

Conversos faced inner conflicts indeed, but that was nothing compared with the reactions of the rest of the populace. Christians as well as Jews had trouble knowing how to deal with these new converts. Should they be welcomed and accepted, or mistrusted and rejected?

The Catholic Church welcomed the *conversos* with open arms, but individual Christians often viewed them with suspicion. "Old Christians," those who had always been Christian, knew that *conversos* were now their brothers and sisters in faith, but knowing that they had been forced into Christianity made it difficult to believe they were genuine. Old Christians were disturbed to see *conversos* filling influential posts and enjoying more privileges than Jews ever had before. Old Christians believed again that people they considered little more than disguised Jews were surpassing them. To make matters worse, many of these New Christians were still practicing Jewish customs. Though these customs (such as avoiding pork) were often related as much to long-standing habits as to any religious convictions, the Old Christians mistrust only increased.

A large part of the Jewish community, too, looked upon the *conversos* with scorn. Though the Jewish population had been greatly reduced in the 1391 pogroms, some Jews had survived the massacres and escaped conversion. Many of these survivors despised those who had converted, seeing them as weaklings who had betrayed their community and their God. They took to calling the *conversos* names like *anusim,* meaning "forced ones," and refused to associate with them. One *converso* who insisted upon attending services at the synagogue was even thrown out by the rest of the congregation. Other Jews were less judgmental. Refusing to turn their backs on their converted friends and relatives, they continued to welcome them into their homes and their community.

Conversos soon felt that their situation was more hazardous than ever before. When they had been Jews, they had faced hostility mainly from Christians. As converts, however, they now faced hostility from Jews as well.

More than ever before, the line between Judaism and Christianity was becoming blurred because the large *converso* class bridged the gap that had formerly separated them. Once again, people feared that Christianity was in danger. Before 1391, Jews and Christians had been relatively easy to identify, and folks found it quite unsettling to suddenly have to keep track of Muslims, Christians, Jews, Christians who acted like Jews, and Jews who pretended to be Christians.

People also feared that *conversos* were at risk of reverting back to Judaism. Most *conversos* had not been properly taught about their new faith at the time of their forced conversion. This missing indoctrination left them especially susceptible to temptation. Therefore, in some towns and cities, various forms of legislation were introduced to enable Christians to easily identify Jews, and thereby to remain separate from them. These laws had a double purpose: to reduce Jewish influence on the *conversos,* and to pressure the unconverted Jews to convert to Christianity.

Some laws forbade Jews to hold office or to possess titles, while others forbade them to practice certain occupations or even to eat, drink, or talk with Christians. In some cities Jews were required to wear an identification badge, while other cities prohibited them from cutting their hair or shaving their beards. Still other legislation prohibited Jews from carrying weapons, wearing fine clothing, or hiring Christians to work for them.

Much of this legislation went unheeded, though. It was largely unenforceable, and the Christian monarchs had bigger concerns, such as keeping their thrones safe from ambitious rivals. Moreover, various popes and other authorities disapproved of these oppressive laws and issued decrees to stop them. Thus, in the two decades following 1391, Jewish people experienced varying amounts of oppression. Many continued to cling to their faith. However, another large conversion took place as the result of a famous debate in 1413, and this time it was voluntary.

The "Disputation of Tortosa," as it was called, was a grand debate set up between a distinguished recent convert, Gerónimo de Santa Fe, and several leading rabbis of Aragon. The discussion lasted almost two years. By its conclusion, thousands more Jews had converted to Christianity in Spain's second historic mass conversion.

For the next several decades, *conversos* settled into their new roles as Christians. Lifelong Christians, however, were not yet ready to accept the former Jews as full Christians, and even the children and grandchildren of converts were referred to as *conversos.* Some converts dropped their Jewish names and adopted Spanish ones, while others embraced

Christianity to the point of becoming priests. One former Jewish rabbi even became the bishop of Burgos.

Relations took a turn for the worse when some *conversos* started acting as if they were better than Old Christians, reasoning that their Jewish heritage linked them directly to Jesus Christ. Some *conversos* proudly called themselves "Christians of Israel," while one man went so far as to refer to Jesus' mother, Mary, as both the "Mother of God" and his "blood relative." This arrogance, though it probably grew out of a need by *conversos* to protect themselves from the disdain of their neighbors, only served to set them further apart from the Christian community. This sense of separateness would later have disastrous consequences.

New Christians returned to their old occupations, and many became wealthy and influential. They were again doctors, financial planners, treasurers, and personal advisers in high positions in Spain's royal households. Wealthy New Christians began to mingle with Old Christians, and eventually they married into Old Christian families. Old Christian families benefited from the wealth that the New Christians brought, and New Christians improved their social standing. Within a few generations, then, most of Spain's Christian aristocracy had some degree of Jewish ancestry, and New Christians had become so successful that they held positions in some of the highest courts in the land.

Iberia at that time was a land divided: its patchwork of kingdoms reflected the political and social divisions of its people. The kingdom of Portugal claimed the lands to the west. The rest of the peninsula was divided into a handful of independent kingdoms with weak ties brought about by royal connections and marriages. Though these kingdoms were collectively known as Spain, they were hardly united by any spirit of nationalism but were, instead, independent domains with their own monarchs, laws, and courts.

Castile, located in the center of the peninsula, was by far

the largest and most powerful kingdom in Spain. To its east lay Aragon. Together the two kingdoms controlled most of the territory in Spain. Another small kingdom, Navarre, lay to the north, and to the south was Granada, the last stronghold of the Moors. While monarchs within these regions continually made and broke political alliances, their subjects were involved in power struggles of their own. This time the struggle concerned Old Christians and *conversos*.

In 1449, Old Christian groups in Toledo, Castile's leading city, held a meeting to discuss the favoritism shown toward Jews and *conversos* by Álvaro de Luna, King Juan II's minister. De Luna had been handling affairs ever since the king had inherited the throne at the age of two. As Old Christians saw things, *conversos* were not true Christians but merely disguised Jews. The group decided that *conversos* should not hold public office, and they drafted a document that would prevent anyone of Jewish descent from holding office or from giving testimony in court. This document, the Sentencia-Estatuto, was approved by the city council.

Pope Nicholas responded with a papal bull, or pope's order, denouncing these prejudices based upon blood origins. He backed up his words by excommunicating all who had helped write the Sentencia-Estatuto. King Juan II was so preoccupied with civil wars that he preferred to mend fences with his subjects. He wrote to the pope asking him to repeal the excommunications. Furthermore, in 1451, the king officially approved the Sentencia-Estatuto and extended it to another city in his realm. Over the next decade, anti-*converso* sentiment grew.

A man with a particularly intense dislike of *Marranos* (a derogatory name of obscure origin that became interchangeable with *conversos*) was Alfonso de Espina. In 1458 he published an influential paper titled "Fortalitium Fidel," which gave rise to the later concept of blood purity. Some scholars say that, surprisingly, Alfonso de Espina

A Spanish painting showing Jews desecrating a Communion wafer. Among some of Spain's Catholics, anti-Semitism ran so deep that even people whose families had converted to Christianity several generations before were eyed with suspicion.

was a convert himself. Though the archbishop of Toledo and other church officials made attempts to stem the tide of hatred, Spanish hearts were hardening against *conversos*.

Within one year of the Sentencia-Estatuto, while political unrest was unraveling the fabric of Spanish society, two royal children were born: Isabel, in Castile, and Fernando, in Aragon. These two children would grow up to be the most influential monarchs in the history of Spain and are today still widely known in English-speaking countries by their anglicized names: Isabella and Ferdinand.

Princess Isabella, half-sister of King Henry IV of Castile, was 17 when Henry named her his direct heir. The following year, 1469, Isabella married Ferdinand, heir to the throne of Aragon. On December 13, 1474, two days after Henry's death, Isabella was crowned queen of Castile. The coronation immediately plunged Castile into a civil war between Isabella's supporters and a group who thought that the monarchy should have passed to Henry's (believed illegitimate) daughter Juana.

At the same time that Isabella was dealing with political turmoil at home, she also became entangled in a quarrel with the pope in Rome. A highly devout and pious Catholic, Isabella recommended some of her trusted priests for positions in Rome. When Pope Sixtus IV instead filled the positions with his relatives and friends, Isabella became indignant. She threatened to cut back on her dealings with the Church and pull all of her royal agents out of Rome. Sixtus IV relented and installed Isabella's priests. But relations between the two remained strained after the incident.

Meanwhile, Spain was still in a state of upheaval. Civil war raged over the throne of Castile, Spaniards were in turmoil over the *conversos,* and the Moors still clung to a small kingdom in the south. During the previous 200 years Christian monarchs, preoccupied with political intrigues and civil unrest, had allowed the Reconquest to stagnate. As long as any Muslim ruler remained on Iberian soil, however, Spain would rest uneasy under the threat of renewed invasion. Isabella and Ferdinand decided that the Moors would have to go, and they knew that it would take the combined strength of a united country to make it happen. The monarchs discussed ways to sew their patchwork of kingdoms into a new nation. They decided to tackle the *converso* problem first.

Several of Isabella's advisers suggested that she set up the Inquisition to deal with the *converso* problem. At first, both Ferdinand and Isabella were reluctant. They counted among their most trusted advisers many *conversos.* The monarchs suspected that prejudice, rather than any actual danger, accounted for much of the turmoil surrounding the *conversos.* Furthermore, Isabella and Ferdinand were not anxious to renew old tensions with the pope. However, some influential anti-*conversos* remained insistent.

Tomás de Torquemada gives Communion to Queen Isabella. The queen's confessor and trusted adviser, Torquemada played a crucial role in convincing the Spanish monarchs to bring the Inquisition to their realm.

Tomás de Torquemada, Isabella's spiritual minister and trusted adviser since she was a girl, urged the monarchs to bring the Inquisition to Spain. He reminded Isabella about her youthful promise to do everything within her power to protect the purity of her faith. Torquemada and other court advisers argued that the Inquisition was the logical answer to the confusion over which converts were true Catholics and which were secret Jews. Headed by intelligent and learned church officials, the Inquisition alone was qualified to make the thorough inquiries required for the identification of heretics. Furthermore, they argued, Isabella's own brother, Henry, had seen the need for this institution. Though nothing had come of it, Henry had requested that Rome set up the Inquisition in Spain around the time of the controversial Sentencia-Estatuto.

Alfonso de Hojeda, head of a monastery in Seville, was convinced of the danger of false converts in his city. When Isabella visited in July of 1477, he pressed her with appeals to establish the Inquisition. After the queen left Seville in October, Hojeda sent her a letter claiming that he had found evidence of a secret meeting of Judaizing *conversos*.

The monarchs finally became convinced. They wrote to Pope Sixtus IV, requesting permission to set up the Inquisition. Sixtus granted the request in a papal bull issued on November 1, 1478. However, the Inquisition wouldn't come to Spain for another two years.

Ferdinand and Isabella wanted to maintain control over how the Inquisition would be run, and they set out to establish their authority with the pope. Remembering Sixtus's tendency to play favorites, the monarchs made it clear that they, not the pope, would be in charge of appointing and dismissing the inquisitors. They also wanted it known that any property confiscated by the Inquisition would become the property of the state, not the Church, as was customary during the medieval Inquisition. Though Sixtus IV disliked these proposals, he feared that another drawn-out dispute with the monarchs would further weaken papal authority, so he agreed. Only a few details remained until the Inquisition could be set in motion, for the monarchs' success would hinge on cementing their authority over their own subjects.

Before Ferdinand and Isabella could unite the country, they needed to present themselves as united, so they agreed to rule as equals. Throughout their close association, they signed documents with the words *"Yo el rey, Yo la reina"* ("I the king, I the queen"). Further strengthening their union was the death of Juan II, making Ferdinand the new king of Aragon. In addition, by the end of 1479, Isabel's side had won the civil war and secured her throne against her niece. The Inquisition could finally be set in motion.

On September 27, 1480, Ferdinand and Isabella appointed the first two official inquisitors. Since religious unrest seemed to be concentrated in the south, that was where the inquisitors would begin their work. In less than a month, residents of Seville learned that inquisitors were headed their way. Having already heard gruesome tales about the Inquisition in other parts of Europe, many of Seville's citizens watched in horror when, in October, a procession of inquisitors and assistants marched into their city to the solemn beat of a drum.

Firestorm Across Spain

In Seville the inquisitors found that nervous citizens, most of them *conversos,* had fled the city, seeking refuge with friends and relatives in other lands. Those who stayed behind were very anxious, but faithful Jews, Moors, and Christians had little to fear from the inquisitors, who were interested only in false *conversos.*

The inquisitors followed centuries-old procedures. They called all the citizens of Seville to a meeting and asked them to report anyone suspected of Judaizing. They also offered a one-month grace period in which those who voluntarily came forward to confess their sins would be given light sentences. Light sentences might entail public whipping (between 100 and 200 lashes was customary), having to wear the dreaded sanbenito, or permanently losing the right to carry a weapon, to use a saddle when riding, or to wear fancy clothes or jewelry.

Though these sentences were light compared with such customary secular punishments as mutilation and branding, citizens were understandably reluctant to come forward. After a few months' time, however, the inquisitors were satisfied with their investigations and were ready to hand down their sentences.

Spain celebrated its first auto-da-fé in Seville on February 6, 1481. Alfonso de Hojeda himself led the ceremony and preached the sermon. Afterward, six men and women became the first official victims of the Spanish Inquisition: they were burned to death. Ironically, Hojeda, who had pressured Isabella to bring the Inquisition to Seville, met his own gruesome death a few days later when the bubonic plague returned.

Seville's two inquisitors continued to be extremely busy, and they soon realized that a tremendous amount of work still needed to be done. In 1482, new inquisitors were appointed, one of whom was Tomás de Torquemada, Isabella's personal confessor.

Torquemada, extremely zealous in his persecution of heretics, was frustrated at the low turnout of citizens willing to report false converts. He knew that they were reluctant to denounce others for fear that friends and families of the accused would retaliate. So Torquemada promised to protect them by keeping their names a secret. Accusations started pouring in.

Torquemada also believed that citizens had trouble recognizing Judaizers, so he made a list of more than 30 clues. For example, potential informers were told to be on the lookout for anyone who wore good clothes on Saturdays (Jewish Sabbath) instead of Sundays, cut the fat from pork or refused to eat pork at all, or put clean sheets on the beds on Saturdays.

Before long, it began to seem as though the eyes and ears of the Inquisition were everywhere. People took to

The emblem of the Spanish Inquisition incorporated the cross, a symbol of the Catholic faith; a sword, symbolizing justice; and a tree branch, symbolizing mercy. The motto read, "Arise, O Lord, and judge thine own cause."

listening at doorways and noting any suspicious or unusual behavior. No one could be trusted, for even the most innocent face might be that of a Judaizer or an informer. Assistants of the inquisitors, called "familiars," went from house to house, checking for signs of Judaizing. *Conversos* began to stock pork in their pantries whether or not they intended to eat it. Familiars also searched for smokeless chimneys on chilly Saturday mornings, since Jewish law forbade Jews to light fires on the Sabbath. *Conversos* were terrified in this atmosphere, and several of them escaped to Rome to lodge a complaint with the pope.

On April 18, 1482, Sixtus IV issued a papal bull that condemned the procedures in Seville and outlined how the inquisitorial process should be conducted. He wrote that

> the Inquisition has for some time been moved not by zeal for the faith and the salvation of souls, but by lust for wealth, and many true and faithful Christians, on the testimony of enemies, rivals, slaves, and other lower and even less proper persons have without any legitimate proof been thrust into secular prisons, tortured and condemned as heretics, and deprived of their goods and property and handed over to the secular arm [the Spanish government] to be executed, to the peril of souls, setting a pernicious example, and causing disgust to many.

Sixtus went on to decree that witnesses should not be anonymous, and that suspects should be permitted to have defense lawyers.

Since the spring of 1482 Ferdinand had been busy concentrating on a new war effort against the Moors' stronghold in Granada, and he resented the pope's intrusion. He responded with a letter insinuating that Sixtus was pro-*converso*—in essence politely telling the pope to mind his own business:

> Things have been told me, Holy Father which, if true, would seem to merit the greatest astonishment. It is said that Your Holiness has granted the conversos a general pardon for all the errors and offences they have committed. . . . To these rumours, however, we have given no credence because they seem to be things which would in no way have been conceded by Your Holiness, who have a duty to the Inquisition. But if by chance concessions have been made through the

persistent and cunning persuasion of the said conversos, I intend never to let them take effect. Take care therefore not to let the matter go further, and to revoke any concessions and entrust us with the care of this question.

Once again, when faced with a challenge to his authority, Sixtus gave in. In effect, this handed over total control of the Inquisition to the Spanish government.

In 1483, Ferdinand and Isabella rewarded Torquemada's zealous work by appointing him inquisitor-general, in charge of coordinating all inquisitorial activities. Torquemada exercised his new power by trying to convince the monarchs to extend the Inquisition into Aragon, though no one knows how much convincing they really needed.

Some historians speculate that Ferdinand may have wanted to expand the Inquisition in order to add to the royal treasury through the confiscation of heretics' property. Isabella, devoted as she was to the defense of her faith, probably regarded it as another opportunity to protect the Catholic religion from dangerous impurities. That the Inquisition was needed in Aragon is questionable; *converso* troubles had been concentrated in Castile. Nevertheless, the monarchs decided to extend the Inquisition into Aragon, a decision that would have profound repercussions for Spain in the succeeding centuries.

Cries of protest echoed from cities all over Aragon when people learned that the Inquisition was on its way. Despite the marriage of their monarchs, Aragon and Castile were still independent of each other, and the people of Aragon resented being made to obey what they considered Castilian authority. Furthermore, they declared that Aragon had no heretics, so the Inquisition was unnecessary. To these arguments the king responded with his own: if there were no heretics in

Aragon, then Aragon need not fear the Inquisition. Many cities in Aragon would later attempt to resist the Inquisition, but none of them would ever match the fame achieved by Teruel.

In 1484, two inquisitors were sent to Teruel to set up the Inquisition. City leaders met them at the gates and refused to allow them to enter. The inquisitors withdrew to a nearby city, then excommunicated the people of Teruel. The clergymen of Teruel appealed to the pope, who defended them with letters releasing them from excommunication.

The inquisitors fought back by declaring that all those who held public office in Teruel were immediately deprived of their jobs. The king supported the inquisitors. He even ordered officials throughout Aragon to take up arms against the citizens of Teruel. Lukewarm response by the Aragonese, however, compelled the king to summon troops from Castile, who gave him their full support. In 1485, Teruel was forced into submission, and many of its leading citizens were burned by the Inquisition for their disobedience.

Many other cities in Aragon also made attempts to resist the dreaded Inquisition. In stubborn cases, however, the king reminded protesters of how Teruel had been ruined when it had dared to disobey. This threat never failed to quiet complaints. Teruel became an example to all that it was useless to oppose the Inquisition.

Desperate *conversos,* however, were not so willing to give up. They could be patient. They would wait for the right opportunity; and when it appeared, they would be ready.

Gaspar Juglar and Pedro Arbués de Epila were inquisitors in Saragossa in 1485. Their dedicated attention to their duties resulted in the execution of *conversos* at several autos-da-fé, which left the *converso* community itching to get even. Leading *conversos,* along with some disgruntled Old Christians, met in secret in the local church. Not only did they want revenge, but they also wanted to get rid of the Inquisition altogether. They reasoned that if they killed the inquisitors, no one else would have the courage to fill their places, and the Inquisition would be finished in Saragossa. They could not have been more mistaken.

If details of the story are accurate, Juglar probably died by poisoning. Following his evening meal, he was seized by sudden, severe stomach cramps, and he died some hours later. His death seems to have had little impact on the community, however.

Following the suspicious death of Juglar, Arbués became concerned for his own safety. He was careful to test everything he ate, he began to wear body armor and a helmet under his monk's robes, and he carried a club for defense. Close to midnight on September 15, 1485, as the monk knelt in prayer in the local church, eight assassins hired by *conversos* crept up behind him. The attack was swift and deadly. One of the assassins landed a blow that crushed his helmet, another slashed his arm, and a third delivered the deathblow—a stab in the back that pierced his neck. Arbues died on September 17. If the *conversos* involved had thought that this violent act would rally the support of the community against the Inquisition, they were terribly shortsighted. In fact, the attack had exactly the opposite effect.

Pedro Arbués was transformed almost overnight from murderer to martyr. People started calling him a saint. Rumors spread that church bells mysteriously rang at the moment of his death and that his blood, still warm and wet on the church stones 12 days after the murder, could be sopped up with handkerchiefs and used to perform miracles.

The biggest changes occurred when the community

Loathed in life, inquisitor Pedro Arbués was venerated in death, as this depiction of his murder reveals. Rather than dealing the Inquisition a blow, Arbués's assassins simply provided it with a martyr.

learned that *conversos* were to blame. Riots broke out in the streets, and mobs gathered to hunt down the assassins as well as their *converso* accomplices. Many were caught within a few days, and each man, tried and condemned by the Inquisition, met his gruesome fate within the year.

The leader of the plot suffered a terrible punishment. His hands were chopped off and nailed to a city door. Afterward he was hanged, taken down while still alive, beheaded, and cut into four pieces, which were displayed throughout the city. The rest of the conspirators met similar fates. The vengeance did not end there, however, and repercussions lasted for years.

Almost a decade later, some of the highest-ranking

members of the king's court, heads of the most influential *converso* families in Spain, were still being implicated and investigated by the Inquisition for their alleged involvement in the conspiracy. It is interesting to note that the king, for reasons that can only be guessed at, protected some of them by granting them immunity from the Inquisition.

The consequences of this single murder cannot be overestimated. Public opinion was radically altered, causing the entire kingdom of Aragon to turn against the *conversos* and to support the Inquisition for the next 100 years. As for the Inquisition in Saragossa, it barely missed a beat. Replacement inquisitors arrived within a week of Arbués's killing and picked up where the murdered inquisitors had left off.

Turmoil continued to roll through Spanish communities, and the next major uproar took place five years later, in 1490. A man was arrested and found to have in his possession what appeared to be a forbidden, blessed Communion wafer. Under grueling questioning the man told a shocking story. He claimed that some *conversos* had told him that they and a number of Jews had crucified a four-year-old Christian boy near the small southern town of La Guardia. They had then cut out his heart for a magic spell against the Christians. Worried officials decided that this problem was too big for them to handle, so they called in Torquemada. About a dozen men were brought before the Inquisition and, under torture, confessed to the crime. Despite the lack of evidence of a body or even a report of a missing child, the men were condemned on the basis of the original man's testimony and their forced confessions. They were publicly executed at an auto-da-fé in November 1491. The trial became famous; reports of the hideous details circulated freely and contributed directly to the catastrophe that soon followed.

The La Guardia trial served to convince the general public what Torquemada had suspected all along: that Jewish influence of any kind was a continuous threat to the Catholic community. Once again, Jews became objects of fear, prejudice, and hate. In Salamanca, even Jewish literature was attacked. Thousands of Hebrew Old Testaments and other religious writings were destroyed in book burnings across the land. The Jews were helpless against this tidal wave of anti-Semitism. This time, though, Jews shared their plight with *conversos,* who, it appeared, would never be forgiven for the sin of having Jewish blood in their veins.

The disorder of the 1480s occurred at the exact time that Ferdinand and Isabella were distracted by their efforts to rid their realm of the Moors. By the end of 1491, though, the fall of Granada appeared certain.

On January 2, 1492, the last Muslim ruler, Boabdil, turned over the keys of the city to the Christians and left Granada forever. Legend has it that on his way through a nearby mountain pass, Boabdil turned for one last look at his beloved city. The name of the pass, *Suspiro del Moro* (Sigh of the Moor), marks the occasion. After 781 years of Muslim occupation, Spain belonged entirely to the Christians. The Reconquest had triumphed at last.

While Ferdinand and Isabella celebrated their victory, Torquemada made an astonishing suggestion. Now that the Moors were no longer a threat, he argued, only the Jews jeopardized the harmony of the nation. Torquemada urged the monarchs to press their advantage immediately. It was time to finish the job of unification. It was time to expel the Jews.

On March 31, 1492, Ferdinand and Isabella signed the Edict of Expulsion, which was announced in all cities on May 1. It had been decreed that the Jewish religion would no longer be permitted

anywhere in the Spanish nation. Of course, conversion was still an option. Jews listened in disbelief as they were told that if they did not convert, they had three months to sell their belongings, pack up, and leave the country.

The monarchs' own Jewish advisers and financiers, Abraham Seneor, Isaac Abravanel, and Meir Melamed, were stunned as well. They offered the monarchs a huge sum of money to repeal the edict. Ferdinand and Isabella

The surrender of Granada, the Muslims' last stronghold in Spain, January 2, 1492. Military victory enabled the Catholic monarchs to turn their attention to the question of what to do with the Jewish and Muslim minorities in their realm.

wavered, undoubtedly thinking of the depleted royal treasury after the long campaign against the Moors. When Torquemada found out about the offer, he reputedly stormed into their chambers. Reminding them that Judas had turned Jesus over in exchange for money, he demanded to know: were they going to do the same? The king and queen turned down the offer.

Once again, thousands of Jews flocked to baptismal fonts, but many more thousands did not. In numbed shock, Jewish families began to prepare for a long, dangerous journey.

Christians and *conversos* alike knew that the Jews had little time in which to prepare. Unscrupulous people took advantage. Debts to the Jews went unpaid, and Jewish possessions sold for a fraction of what they were worth. Jews also learned, to their dismay, that they would not be allowed to take any gold, silver, or jewels out of the country. Those who could entrust their land and property to the safekeeping of *converso* relatives did so. Others were forced to accept whatever the Christians offered in exchange. By the middle of summer, thousands of Jewish families, carrying what was left of their belongings on their shoulders, straggled toward the borders.

Two weeks after Ferdinand and Isabella signed the Edict of Expulsion, the monarchs found themselves listening to the persistent pleas of a Genoese sailor as he outlined his incredible plan to reach the Far East—and thereby gain access to the profitable trade in spices and silk—by sailing west. Isabella and Ferdinand reluctantly gave their permission and, with the financial backing of their Jewish courtiers, outfitted him with some ships and provisions.

The sailor, Christopher Columbus, set out on his now-famous voyage of discovery on August 3, 1492.

Ironically, this voyage—financed by Spain's Jews, undertaken with Jewish sailors, and, some speculate, led by a person possibly of Jewish ancestry—set sail two days after Spain's Jews trickled away from their beloved ancestral homeland.

Quenching the Flames

7

Indescribable suffering was in store for Spain's expelled Jews. Few countries in Europe would accept them, and many of them forbade Jews to cross their lands. Traveling north was not an option either. Most of the countries in western Europe had expelled their Jews long before this: England, in 1290; France, in 1306 and 1490; and Germany, in the 12th century and in 1348.

Many Jews traveled west to Portugal, where the king gave them permission to stay six months. As soon as their time expired, however, the treacherous king enslaved them and stole their children. Jewish children as young as two years old were torn from their parents' arms and shipped off as slaves to colonize the island of São Tomé, off the coast of Africa, where three-fourths of them died.

Jews who traveled southward to Africa and westward across the Mediterranean Sea to the Ottoman Empire in the east fared little better. They suffered storms, starvation, drowning, disease, enslavement, and betrayal. The king of a northern Sahara tribe, after welcoming a group of Jews, is reputed to have ended up butchering them. Hearing rumors that the Jews had swallowed gold coins to smuggle them out of Spain, he ordered that their stomachs be ripped open in search of the treasure.

Of the Jews who survived these dangers, many decided that it would be better to face baptism at home than death abroad. Thousands straggled back into Spain, accepted baptism, and were welcomed with enthusiasm. In many cases their land and property were given back, and they resumed their lives as New Christians.

Historians have long attempted to understand why Ferdinand and Isabella chose to expel the Jews. Many theories have been offered, but the evidence fails to conclusively prove any one.

The decision to expel was probably not motivated by economic gain, since the monarchs were well aware of the many essential services that the Jews provided to Spain. The monarchs themselves stood to lose considerably because many of their closest advisers—and even their own personal physicians—were Jewish.

Nor was personal prejudice a likely cause; Isabella was well known as a protector of Jews. In 1477, for example, she extended her protection to the Jewish community in Trujillo, saying, "All the Jews in my realms are mine and under my care and protection, and it belongs to me to defend and aid them and keep justice."

Perhaps the monarchs, well aware of the rising tide of anti-Semitic feelings in their realm, thought that the threat of expulsion would convince most of Spain's remaining Jews to convert. Thousands of Jews did convert: even an 80-year-old court financier, Abraham Seneor, converted to Catholicism. Nevertheless, the king and queen severely underestimated the Jews' dedication to their faith, because thousands chose exile over baptism.

Some historians have even gone so far as to propose that the monarchs realized they could no longer protect the Jews in their realm from the wrath of the Christians. Maybe they thought it best to remove the Jews from harm's way. Furthermore, as several historians have noted, it was safer for the monarchs to ride the wave of anti-Semitism than to have it crash down over them.

Isabella's own words give us a glimpse into her thinking. When asked by some Jews about her decision, she is reported to have replied, "The king's heart is in the hand of the Lord, as the rivers of water. God turneth it withersoever He will. Do you believe that this comes upon you from us? The Lord hath put this thing into the heart of the king."

Her words certainly suggest the most convincing theory of all—that the decision was made for religious reasons and that it was the king who was the driving force behind it. Perhaps the wording of the edict itself explains it best, citing as its main reason "the great harm suffered by Christians [that is, *conversos*] from the contact, intercourse and communication which they have with the Jews, who always attempt in various ways to seduce faithful Christians from our Holy Catholic Faith." The monarchs concluded that "the only solution to all these ills is to separate the said Jews completely from contact with Christians, and expel them from all our realms."

Following the expulsion of the Jews, Torquemada, though he was 72 years old, continued his work with unquenched zeal. His passion for the elimination of false converts never died. Surprisingly, Torquemada himself probably had Jewish ancestry. His grandfather is believed to have married a converted Jew when it was the fashion for Old Christians and New Christians to join status with wealth. Pope Alexander VI appointed four new inquisitors to share Torquemada's position; they assisted Torquemada and restrained his excesses. Torquemada died at the age of 78 in 1498.

In 1499, the monarchs turned their attention to the last remaining religious minority in their realm: the Moors. Since 1492, when control of Granada had passed to the Christians, the Muslims there had ceased to enjoy their own kingdom, but instead became a minority under Christian rule. Although conquered Moors at the time of the surrender had been permitted to leave the country, most had chosen to stay because of the lenient terms of the takeover—terms that allowed conquered Moors to keep their religious and cultural identities. These terms were violated when Isabella and Ferdinand decided to begin a campaign to convert the Muslims. Despite the efforts of such enlightened clergymen as Hernando de Talavera— who advocated respect for Islamic culture, the use of the Arabic language in preaching, and conversion through gentle persuasion—conversions were usually forced.

Granada's Moors strongly resented the situation. They were outraged when their mosque was turned into a church, and violent revolts took place all over the Spanish realm. Nevertheless, the baptisms continued.

By 1501, the crown could note with satisfaction that most of Granada's Moors had finally converted. Converted Moors were now known as *Moriscos,* "Moorish" Christians who, though now technically of the same faith as the Spanish majority, still faced prejudice because of their Islamic ways.

In October 1501, Granada's vast collection of Arabic books was condemned to the flames of a massive bonfire. Many of these books came from the magnificent libraries built during the time of Granada's golden age of *convivencia.* Their destruction erased for all time some of the finest collections of scholarship and learning the Western world had ever known.

In 1502, Ferdinand and Isabella stunned the remaining

unconverted Moors by offering them the same choice they had earlier offered the Jews: convert or leave the country. The Moors, having witnessed the disastrous results of the Jewish exodus in 1492, were reluctant to repeat the experience. By midcentury almost all of Spain's remaining Moors had converted and were, more or less, living peacefully with their Old Christian neighbors. However, since cultural habits are difficult to erase, Moriscos continued to cling to their Islamic customs and to be subjected to intense pressure by some of the Christian clergy and the general public.

A pivotal pronouncement from an Islamic leader in North Africa seemed to aid the Spanish Moriscos with their conflict. He declared that in times of persecution Muslims could outwardly conform to Christianity while

This 16th-century bas-relief depicts a mass baptism of Muslims. Having seen the sorrows that befell Jews expelled from Spain, many Moors chose to convert to Catholicism—or at least to feign conversion.

still staying true to their beliefs. Although this ruling came as a relief to devout Moriscos, it actually endangered them further, because it encouraged the practice of heresy. The Inquisition moved in to investigate such charges as Muslims dancing, playing music at night, or eating the traditional African dish couscous.

The Morisco revolt of 1568 and the ensuing savage war was the turning point in the relationship between the Christian and Morisco communities. Unspeakable atrocities committed by both sides seemed to remove forever the possibility of peaceful coexistence.

By the 1580s the discovery of several Morisco plots to support another Muslim invasion from North Africa sealed the Moriscos' fate. Official opinion turned completely against them. On April 4, 1609, despite many cities' claims that their Moriscos were true and loyal Christians, an edict was signed for their expulsion. The expulsion, which took place in stages, was completed by 1615.

With the expulsion of the Moors, Spain's rulers had finally succeeded in their aim of uniting the nation under one faith. This unity came at a steep price, however; for by ridding the land of the Jews and the Moors, Spain effectively wiped out two of the three main communities whose partnership had contributed to the greatness of the enlightened *convivencia* era.

Meanwhile, back in the first two decades of the 16th century, while the Inquisition was busily engaged in the Morisco turbulence, it had also been called upon to investigate rumors coming from overseas. From that point on, the Inquisition's activities would extend beyond the shores of Spain.

Columbus's discovery of the New World had inspired a wave of Spanish exploration and colonization, first in the Caribbean and then on the mainland of Central and South America. Gold and silver from the colonies poured into

Spain, financing further growth and helping to create a vast empire.

Soon, however, authorities in Spain became convinced that inquisitors were needed across the Atlantic. Jews had been officially banned from entering Spain's New World colonies, but many *conversos* had managed to establish themselves there. Again, though some converts were true Catholics, many were disguised Jews who immediately reverted to Judaism once they were free of the Inquisition's grasp. Spain was not about to let this go unchallenged. In 1519, shortly after Hernán Cortés landed in Mexico, the New World's first inquisitors were appointed to find and punish false converts, or so-called Crypto-Jews. Mexico City's first auto-da-fé took place nine years later, in 1528.

Around the same time that Spain was crossing frontiers in the New World, intellectuals in the Spanish nation—spurred by the writings of some of Europe's enlightened thinkers—began to explore new frontiers of thought as well. One influential Spaniard was a man by the name of Juan Luis Vives.

At the age of 16, Vives, the child of secretly Judaizing *conversos,* was sent out of Spain to escape the Inquisition, which was then actively pursuing Crypto-Jews. He studied in Paris and served for a time as a professor of Humanities at Louvain, later moving to England to become the teacher of Mary, Princess of Wales. While in England he held a post at Oxford, where he lectured on philosophy. Vives lost the English king's favor and was jailed for six weeks when he openly opposed Henry VIII's divorce from Catherine of Aragon. Afterward, Vives left England for the Netherlands to devote the rest of his life to writing. Among his most notable ideas were those related to religion, social reform, and education. For example, Vives advocated the use of native languages in schools, the building of academies, and education for women, as well as social reforms such as the humane treatment of the mentally ill and better care for the poor.

The ideas of Vives and other philosophers spread throughout western Europe through their writings and began to challenge the very foundations of social structure, religion, and the Catholic Church. This was the time of the birth and growth of Protestantism.

Spain reacted to Protestantism in a predictable manner —labeling it another dangerous heresy and unleashing the Inquisition against this new enemy. The first Protestant victim of the Inquisition, Francisco de San Román, was burned at the stake in 1540.

Though Spanish officials fought hard to keep their country safe from what they considered dangerous beliefs, the ideas of reformers proved impossible to suppress. The invention of the printing press with moveable type led to an information explosion by making books widely available. Previously, books—which had to be copied by hand—were rare and too expensive for wide distribution. Thanks to the printing press, literature flowed freely across Spain's borders, bringing with it new ideas and the fresh scent of change.

Officers of the Inquisition reacted, making books their next target. The Spanish government attempted to purge the country of any written materials deemed dangerous. The first printed Index of Banned Books listed 16 authors, leaders of Europe's reform movement. That index, however, was only one of several. In 1559, Fernando de Valdes, with limited help from his friend Melchor Cano, compiled another list of banned books. His Index of Prohibited Books included books and authors condemned by the Inquisition, materials written by heretical leaders, anything that contained an anti-Catholic slant, and books on magic. Even vernacular (native language) translations of the Bible were banned because authorities worried that the uneducated might misinterpret confusing passages if they read the

The printing press, shown here in a 16th-century engraving, led to a proliferation of relatively inexpensive books, making it next to impossible for Inquisition authorities to muzzle reformers.

Bible themselves. It was safer, the authorities felt, to leave biblical interpretation and explanation to the clergy, so only Latin Bibles were permitted.

Foreign books were banned, and books printed in Spain had to be approved by the government. Booksellers were forced to turn over their entire inventories for inspection, and authorities detained ships in port to search their cargoes. Some books had passages crudely cut or blotted out with ink, while others were completely destroyed. Determined people still managed to obtain forbidden works, because books easily crossed the poorly patrolled borders. Furthermore, the ideas of enlightened thinkers, once rooted, grew and blossomed over the centuries into revolutionary concepts. These very concepts would eventually bring an end to the dreaded Spanish Inquisition.

Fire Prevention

The destruction—by the French—of the Office of the Inquisition in Barcelona is greeted with jubilation. Napoleon's invasion had the indirect result of weakening the power of the Catholic Church in Spain, although the Inquisition would return several times before being permanently abolished in 1834.

T he Spanish Inquisition did not die a quick death. Gradually, however, ideas that questioned the traditional social, religious, and political order sparked revolutions in other lands. The influence of these revolutions, in turn, enabled Spain to finally emerge from the pall of oppression and prejudice.

American colonists used the concepts of human equality, tolerance, and liberty born in western Europe to draft the Declaration of Independence in 1776. In turn, the success of the American Revolution inspired French people to throw off the yoke of monarchy through the French Revolution of 1789.

In 1808 Napoleon Bonaparte of France invaded Spain, captured Madrid, and forced the Spanish king, Ferdinand VII, to renounce his throne. Napoleon installed his brother, Joseph Bonaparte, as king of Spain, but the Spanish and their British and Portuguese allies resisted. One indirect result of this conflict, called the Peninsular War, was the creation of the Spanish Liberal Constitution of March 19, 1812, which was the first of many tiny steps toward the establishment of religious freedom in Spain. This constitution listed reforms designed to decrease the Catholic Church's political influence and wealth, but at the same time it also claimed that the Roman Catholic faith was, and always would be, Spain's religion.

In 1813 the Inquisition was abolished, but after Napoleon's defeat in 1814 and King Ferdinand VII's return to the Spanish throne, the Inquisition also returned. Over the next two decades, the Inquisition was abolished and restored several times. Finally, on July 15, 1834, Ferdinand's fourth wife, María Cristina, abolished the Inquisition for the last time. Never again would the Inquisition condemn another poor soul to the flames.

Though the Inquisition was officially gone, Spain wasn't ready to fully support the concept of freedom of religion. Only after another 100 years of gradual reforms and new constitutions would Spain adopt complete religious freedom. In 1837 the constitution claimed merely to support Roman Catholicism; in 1856 religious liberty was introduced, with the stipulation that non-Catholics could profess their beliefs, but not worship publicly; in 1860 distinctions between "New" and "Old" Christians were officially abolished; by 1869 all people were guaranteed the right to public and private worship; in 1876 the constitution called for freedom of speech, religion, and assembly; and the constitutions of 1931 and 1978 approved the complete separation of church and state by abolishing the concept of a "state religion" and granting full religious freedom to all.

■　　■　　■

Over the years, the unusual circumstances surrounding the Spanish Inquisition have continued to be a source of interest and controversy. Historians have studied the existing records, statistics, and personal accounts. As a result of some individuals' inaccuracies or personal biases, as well as the aura of secrecy with which the Inquisition surrounded itself, these studies have given rise to a body of misconceptions about the Spanish Inquisition, known as the "Inquisition Myth," or the "Black Legend."

Over the years the number of victims of the Spanish Inquisition has frequently been exaggerated. Such wildly differing numbers as 30,000 executions, 300,000 executions, and even 3 million executions have been cited. Many modern historians, examining Spain's population during the Inquisition period, believe that the number of deaths had to have been much lower. Maybe the mistaken inclusion of effigies and human remains partially accounts for the higher death totals.

In the 356 years in which it operated, the Spanish Inquisition is believed to have been responsible for the deaths of between 1 and 2 percent of those it investigated, or between 2,000 and 3,000 people. In addition, though the Inquisition lasted for more than three and a half centuries, roughly three-fourths of its activities took place in its first 50 years. The rest of the time, except for small bursts of activity in response to arising crises, the number of investigations and executions remained relatively small. In actuality, the outrageous activities of the Spanish Inquisition were mirrored—and at times magnified—by similar activities in most of the other western European countries. In fact, there seems to be one major difference between the medieval Inquisition of France, Germany, and Italy and the more famous one known as the Spanish

Echoes of infamy: Hooded penitents march in a Holy Week procession in modern-day Spain, their costumes mirroring those worn by executioners during the Spanish Inquisition.

Inquisition. The medieval Inquisition always remained under the power of the Church, whereas the Spanish Inquisition operated outside of papal control. The reason the Inquisition will forever be linked with Spain is that Ferdinand and Isabella adopted it and controlled it according to their own beliefs and for their own ends.

People today denounce the medieval Inquisitions for their unfair procedures: acceptance of testimony from secret and unreliable witnesses, lack of defense lawyers, lengthy waits for trial, confiscation of property even before conviction, use of torture, encouragement of accusations by neighbors and family members, and the terrible practice of punishing children and grandchildren for the sins of their parents. At the time, however, many people accepted such procedures as valid and necessary; the concept of defendants' rights was unknown.

Ironically, the Spanish Inquisition rarely played favorites. Its list of victims, whether young or old, male or female, included philosophers, criminals, saints, scientists, heretics, Jews, Muslims, Protestants, English people, practitioners of witchcraft, and even books—in short, anyone whose ideas differed from those held by the Inquisition authorities.

Some of the most lasting damage, however, was inflicted on the Spanish mind and spirit, which for years was stifled by the concept of *limpieza de sangre,* or blood purity. Oppressive statutes required proof of freedom from accusations of heresy by the Inquisition—as well as freedom from the taint of Jewish blood as far back as three generations—before applicants would be awarded marriage licenses or entry into some colleges and posts. Some Spaniards, uncertain of their family history, decided not to apply for high-level posts or even to marry. In the oppressive times, Spaniards were right to fear the discovery of Jewish links in their family chain.

There were no fiery explosions to mark the end of the Spanish Inquisition; it simply ran out of fuel, its final curls of smoke drifting away on the winds of reform. Yet even today the embers of ignorance, intolerance, and fear, which fueled the Spanish Inquisition, continue to glow. These destructive forces will not cease to haunt humanity until we learn to recognize the danger and snuff out the embers before they burst into flames.

Chronology

613	The Visigoth king Sisebut proclaims Christianity the only religion permitted in Spain and forces Jews to convert to Christianity.
711	Muslims from North Africa invade Spain and sweep unchecked across the Iberian Peninsula.
1348	Bubonic plague, called the "Black Death," devastates Spain. Jews are suspected of plots to destroy Christianity.
1391	Violent mobs massacre or forcibly convert thousands of Jews in pogroms that begin in Granada and radiate across Spain.
1413	The Disputation of Tortosa convinces thousands of Jews to voluntarily convert to Christianity.
1478	Pope Sixtus IV issues a papal bull on November 1 granting Ferdinand and Isabella permission to set up the Inquisition in Spain.
1480	Ferdinand and Isabella appoint the first two inquisitors for Seville.
1483	Tomás de Torquemada is appointed inquisitor-general for all of Spain.
1485	The murder of inquisitor Pedro Arbués by *conversos* unexpectedly sparks support for the Inquisition.
1490	La Guardia trial for the rumored crucifixion of a Christian child by *conversos* convinces the Spanish monarchs of the need for further action.
1492	On January 2, Granada falls to Christian forces, completing the seven-century Reconquest. The Edict of Expulsion, signed by the monarchs on March 31, offers Jews the choice of being baptized or leaving the country. On August 3, Christopher Columbus sets sail on his first voyage of discovery.
1502	Another edict forces Muslims to choose between baptism and exile.
1609	Moriscos (Moorish Christians) are expelled from Spain beginning on April 4.

Chronology

1812	Spanish Liberal Constitution begins gradual move toward separation of the Catholic Church and the state.
1813	First official attempt to abolish the Inquisition occurs, though it is later reinstated.
1834	On July 15, Queen Mother María Cristina officially abolishes the Inquisition.
1860	Distinctions between "New" and "Old" Christians are officially abolished.
1869	Spanish Constitution guarantees the right to public and private worship.
1876	Spanish Constitution calls for freedom of speech, religion, and assembly.
1931, 1978	Constitutions approve complete separation of church and state, abolish the concept of a state religion, and grant full religious freedom to all.

Further Reading

Bowker, John. *World Religions.* New York: Dorling Kindersley, 1997.

Braziller, George, in association with The Jewish Museum. *Convivencia: Jews, Muslims, and Christians in Medieval Spain,* ed. by Vivian B. Mann, et al. New York: The Jewish Museum, 1992.

Chaliand, Gerard, and Jean-Pierre Rageau. *The Penguin Atlas of Diasporas.* New York: Penguin, 1995.

Clare, John D., ed. *Fourteenth-Century Towns.* Orlando, Fla.: Harcourt Brace and Co., 1996.

Descola, Jean. *A History of Spain,* trans. by Elaine P. Halperin. New York: Alfred A. Knopf, 1962.

Kamen, Henry. *The Spanish Inquisition: A Historical Revision.* New Haven, Conn.: Yale University Press, 1998.

Konstam, Angus. *Atlas of Medieval Europe.* New York: Checkmark Books, 2000.

Lea, Henry Charles. *The Inquisition of the Middle Ages: Its Organization and Operation.* London: Eyre & Spottiswoode, 1963.

Nardo, Don. *Life on a Medieval Pilgrimage.* San Diego: Lucent Books, 1996.

Netanyahu, B. *Toward the Inquisition.* Ithaca, N.Y., and London: Cornell University Press, 1997.

Nicolle, David. *Medieval Knights.* New York: Viking Children's Press, 1997.

Peters, Edward. *Inquisition.* New York: The Free Press, 1988.

Roth, Cecil. *The Spanish Inquisition.* New York: W. W. Norton and Co., 1996.

Shannon, Albert C., O.S.A. *The Medieval Inquisition.* Collegeville, Minn.: The Order of Saint Benedict, Inc., 1991.

Further Reading

Stewart, Gail B. *Life During the Spanish Inquisition.* San Diego: Lucent Books, 1998.

Turberville, A. S. *Medieval Heresy and the Inquisition.* London: Archon Books, 1964.

Wingate, Philippa. *The Usborne Book of Kings and Queens from Tutankhamen to Elizabeth II.* London: Usborne Publishing, Ltd., 1995.

Index

Index

Index

Picture Credits

SUSAN McCARTHY MELCHIORE lives in Newtown Square, Pennsylvania, with her husband and three children. She studied foreign languages at West Chester University, where she graduated with honors with a degree in Spanish Education. She has done graduate work in Education, Sociolinguistics, and French. She taught for six years in the Pennsylvania school system before leaving to raise her growing family and to begin writing seriously. This is her second book for Chelsea House.

JILL McCAFFREY has served for four years as national chairman of the Armed Forces Emergency Services of the American Red Cross. Ms. McCaffrey also serves on the board of directors for Knollwood—the Army Distaff Hall. The former Jill Ann Faulkner, a Massachusetts native, is the wife of Barry R. McCaffrey, who served in President Bill Clinton's cabinet as director of the White House Office of National Drug Control Policy. The McCaffreys are the parents of three grown children: Sean, a major in the U.S. Army; Tara, an intensive care nurse and captain in the National Guard; and Amy, a seventh grade teacher. The McCaffreys also have two grandchildren, Michael and Jack.